# New Zealand Native
# GROUND COVER
# PLANTS

A practical guide for gardeners and landscapers

First published in 2014 by
CANTERBURY UNIVERSITY PRESS
University of Canterbury
Private Bag 4800, Christchurch
NEW ZEALAND
www.cup.canterbury.ac.nz

ISBN 978-1-927145-61-6

A catalogue record for this book is available from the National Library of New Zealand

Cover and page design and layout by Book Design Ltd, Christchurch
Typeset in Adobe Garamond Pro 10.5/14.5pt
Cover images: *Hebe* ✕*franciscana* 'Lobelioides' and *Acaena caesiiglauca*

Printed by Choice Printing Inc, Taipei, Taiwan

# New Zealand Native
# GROUND COVER
# PLANTS

A practical guide for gardeners and landscapers

## Lawrie Metcalf | Roy Edwards

CANTERBURY UNIVERSITY PRESS

# Contents

# Introduction

Any disturbed ground is soon covered by plants. They arise from a host of seeds or spores, either from the soil seed bank or that are transported there by various means. Often the species that grow in such ground are colonising weeds. Left alone, after this first flourishing, larger, soft-wooded perennials appear, followed by sub-shrubs, woody shrubs and, eventually, trees. This is the process of natural succession.

In a garden we try to control our patch by designing plantings that are both aesthetically pleasing and functional. By functional we mean that the planted areas are relatively maintenance free, the need for mowing and for inputs such as fertilising and spraying for pests and diseases are reduced or eliminated, and, most importantly, the chosen plants do not impede access down paths, block views, or shade the sun during the cooler months when it is most needed.

The careful use of New Zealand native plants as ground cover is a way of reducing maintenance in gardens of all sizes while producing an aesthetically pleasant environment. Like other forms of gardening, ground cover planting will be most satisfying when the garden is properly planned and the plants are carefully chosen to fit the design objectives and the scale of the area to be planted.

Along with good planning and plant selection, a crucial part of creating a satisfying garden is preparing the area. Good soil preparation

Left: Formal arrangement of New Zealand native plants, including ground covers, at Broadfield NZ Landscape Garden near Christchurch.

and eradication of as many weeds as possible before planting – especially perennial weeds – will save a lot of maintenance later. Using ground cover plants will reduce maintenance, but it will not eliminate it. As well as reducing the weed bank before planting, eliminating weeds during the establishment phase and removing unwanted seedlings after your plants have established are the main ingredients for successful ground cover gardens.

There is an increasing momentum for the use of native plants in gardens throughout New Zealand, but sometimes it appears as if little thought is given to the type of plant in relation to the site and the objectives for the garden. Making the wrong choices often leads to a garden that is planted with enthusiasm, only to be removed a few years later because the area has become overgrown, or because the plants are too large or unsuitable for the site.

The aim of this book is to enhance understanding of plant choice based on the way plants grow and cover the ground. Knowing how ground cover plants can be used in a garden will help to achieve the goal of reducing maintenance while providing a satisfying vista. The second part of this book comprises a list of suitable ground cover plants, this not only includes species but also takes into account the continuing development of hybrids and cultivars that are now available to gardeners.

Although there is a large body of literature available on re-vegetation techniques relating to biodiversity and species survival, this is of little relevance to the gardener seeking to select plants to fulfil a variety of functions in the smaller, garden setting. When selecting suitable plants, there are several factors the gardener must take into consideration. Seedlings can be an unknown quantity: some may perform well and some may prove to be quite unsatisfactory. Some species that are fairly uniform in their growth form and appearance can be chosen with confidence that they will perform well. However, for other species, choosing suitable plants for garden use is easier if the plants have been produced clonally and their characteristics are known. For this reason, many of the newer and existing hybrids and cultivars may be preferable where a specific habit or foliage colour, or plants of a known vigour, are required. We hope that this book will provide guidance on these aspects of gardening with New Zealand ground cover plants.

Right: *Coprosma repens.*

# What is a ground cover plant?

## The battle for resources

All plants cover and shade the ground to some extent, even deciduous plants. Plants orient their leaves to maximise light interception in order to grow. In this sense, any plant could be described as ground cover. In nature, plants of all sorts and sizes compete with each other for light and space, adapting to changes in ascendancy with their competitors and to changes in the environment between the days, weeks, seasons and years of their existence. Nothing is ever static between the competing plants and the ever-changing environment. The battle between plants for resources never ends.

Over time, some plants have developed the ability to climb in order to compete with the larger trees, while others have adapted by becoming shade tolerant or by developing the ability to colonise new ground rapidly, only later to be overgrown by something larger. Plants will adapt and use whatever their strategic advantages are in order to compete for the essential resources for growth: light, moisture, carbon dioxide, nutrients and space.

Left: *Polystichum richardii*.

The fast-growing carpet former *Acaena caesiiglauca* (front) is in competition for light and other resources with the larger spreader *Libertia peregrinans* (rear).

Plants that are cultivated by you, the gardener, are also eventually going to compete with other plants around them. Most perennial plants, in order to survive, have to incrementally add new tissue, and so inevitably they continue to grow larger. However, in a garden, you can affect the growth and competitive strategies of any particular plant or group of plants through activities such as weeding, pruning, altering the spacing between plants and plant selection.

If the aim for a garden is to try to mimic nature, it will inevitably involve the use of ground cover plants to some extent. However, bear in mind that the effort to mimic nature is often based on the assumption that the natural environment is static. In reality, the scene in nature is an ever-evolving picture. It may be a relatively fast or slow process of change depending on growth rates, or it can alter dramatically if catastrophic events such as a major storm affect the balance of power among the plants. Another aim might be simply to reduce maintenance or to create an aesthetically pleasant place.

In a garden it is not just the plants we decide to grow that we need to focus on. There are other factors that work against all gardeners. The point was well made by Alexander Pope in 1731 in his epistle to Lord Burlington:

"In all, let nature never be forgot … Consult the genius of the place in all … That tells the waters to rise or fall … Now breaks, or now directs th' intending lines … Paints as you plant, and as you work, designs."

Perhaps Pope was in part alluding to the unrelenting competition from weeds, which will be dealt with later, but also to the relative speeds of growth and competition between different plants and the way in which they spread to cover the ground, making their own impact on the original design. Others may, of course, interpret this quote differently.

## A different kind of gardening

So, while you should determine how best you can prepare, plant and maintain your garden for any particular design objective, you will need to be adaptable and prepared to make subtle or essential changes along the way, accepting that a garden is always a work in progress. The use of ground cover plants is a way of gardening that can reward minimal effort, if you get the basics right. It probably spells an end to higher-maintenance gardening, including the rejection of some of the more commonly grown, short-term-display, high-maintenance plants.

It may also mean that you can reject some of the other aspects of the garden industry that have become 'essentials' for many. Do you really need to apply those fertilisers or spray those garden pests? Why do you need to install those irrigation systems? Would watering to get plants established suffice? Have you noticed that in nature these so-called 'essentials' so often publicised in newspapers and magazines are not required at all? If you choose plants that are well suited to your local area they are likely to be hardy and perform well without too much extra cost or high-end maintenance.

*Poa cita* (silver tussock) form the natural ground cover (foreground), while the planted forest of pines form a larger scale of ground cover in the background.

If we accept that plants of all shapes and sizes, from the largest trees down to the smallest herbaceous plants, cover the ground to a greater or lesser extent, then what constitutes ground cover comes down to a matter of scale. A motorway embankment can include large trees and shrubs, while a garden for an ownership flat or an over-sixties unit is likely to include only small or lower-growing ground cover plants. The same low-growing plants would be completely out of scale next to a multi-storied building.

In the conventional sense, ground cover planting is based on the use of low-growing plants, usually less than 30 cm or so in height. These plants are often mass planted in groups, designed to create a harmonious picture based on their textural qualities, colour and so on. Ground cover plants are often spreading or carpeting types of plants. For example, a mass planting of *Pittosporum tenuifolium* (kōhūhū) or similar species will effectively cover the ground and look appropriate in a park or similar situation.

Clump-forming *Carex*, *Anemanthele* and *Phormium* species, with the much taller *Cordyline* at the rear, provide an attractive soft edge to the contemporary architecture behind.

It is up to you to plan for your particular location. It is not the scale of the plants in relation to human size that is the main consideration, but the scale of the place in which they are to grow. It is a measure of the skill of a good gardener to choose plants correctly, so that, for example, large evergreen trees do not adversely affect your neighbour's quality of life, especially when planting in small sections in urban areas. Equally, the planting for a motorway or large park should be on a grand scale to reflect the space involved. Provided the nature of the space is taken into consideration and the objectives involved in the overall design are met, what constitutes a ground cover plant is simply any plant that can be used to suit your purpose, based on the scale of the operation.

However, bearing in mind the limitations of a book such as this, ground cover plants have been chosen with smaller gardens in mind, and therefore include plants that generally will not grow to more than about a metre in height.

## Habit of growth

Plants compete for light, nutrients and moisture in a garden, and they utilise different strategies to occupy space. Some plants, by their habit of growth, are particularly suited to being used as ground cover plants. You can exploit the way these plants grow to cover the ground to best effect in your garden. In order to do so, it is useful to consider the different ways that plants achieve this.

As already mentioned, in nature there is a gradual succession of plants, from the very small colonisers to the climax forest of very large trees. Ground cover plants may initially be carpeting mosses or liverworts, but these are gradually replaced by grasses, annuals, ferns or low-growing, soft-wooded perennial plants, and ultimately by larger woody shrubs, climbers and trees. So, in a garden we should be aware that very low-growing ground cover plants will be subject to larger invaders continually trying to establish. It may be better in some cases to avoid the very low-growing plants and concentrate on choosing slightly taller plants, making maintenance of the garden that much easier.

There are a number of accepted categories that describe the habit of growth of different ground cover plants. The English horticulturist Graham Thomas, in his book on plants for ground covers published in the 1970s, described the modes of growth for plants used as ground cover. Another English horticulturist, Frederick Boddy, published a book about the same time called *Groundcover and Other Ways to Weed-free Gardens.*

Boddy dealt largely with the different ways weeds spread to occupy space and their respective modes of growth. Both Boddy and Thomas used similar terms to describe how plants spread.

We follow the classification system of Boddy and Thomas, and in addition have included one further category to deal with rosette-forming plants, which do not easily fit into any of their categories.

# The classification of ground cover plants

Note that although these categories can generally be relied on, occasionally some species may appear to fit into more than one category, often when grown under different environmental conditions.

## Carpet or mat formers

Plants that are more or less uniform in height and texture, or that have a prostrate habit of growth, often layering as they grow and spreading across the ground.

## Sprawlers

Plants that have a more or less uneven texture and a loose habit of growth. Shoots produced are often erect, and on reaching a tipping point bend down to the ground and layer themselves, then repeat the process.

Carpet former
*Pimelea urvilleana.*

Carpet former or sprawler
*Coprosma X kirkii* 'Kirkii'.

## Hummock formers

Best described as social plants, hummock formers are more or less round
or bun shaped and often useful as a barrier against faster-growing and
more invasive species. As the plants grow together they form a barrier to
lower-growing ground cover plants.

Hummock former *Leonohebe
cupressoides.*

## Clump formers

Plants that are variable in height and tend to increase in width from the base. A number of well-known New Zealand native plants such as flax (*Phormium*) fall into this category.

## Spreaders

Plants that are more or less uniform in height and texture and spread by underground shoots (rhizomes). This group can be more of a challenge to manage in a garden, as daughter plants can pop up some distance away from the mother plant at the end of rhizomes. The use of larger hummock formers can help keep this group confined to the areas where you want them.

Left: Clump former *Phormium tenax* in the foreground and *Cyathea medullaris* at the rear.

Below: Spreader *Libertia peregrinans*, showing the pop-up nature of the way this species spreads by underground rhizomes.

Rosette former *Celmisia spectabilis.*

## Rosette formers

These plants do not easily fit into any of the categories above. In some cases they may appear to act like carpet formers, in others they may grow quite tall. Rosette formers are plants that normally produce leaves that radiate out from the centre, like a lawn dandelion. They usually form from a tap root and will naturally spread by seed.

## Plant names

Botanical names are written according to the International Code of Botanical Nomenclature and follow certain conventions. The same botanical names are used by botanists, horticulturists and other professionals all over the world. The scientific name of a plant usually consists of two parts (the genus and the species). Collectively these are called the binomial name. Binomial names are written in italics (or underlined) to differentiate them from other names. The generic name always begins with an upper-case letter and the specific name with a lower-case letter. The generic name is akin to a person's surname and the specific name to their first name (e.g. Smith John or *Coprosma robusta*). Within the genus *Coprosma*, just as there may be many other Smiths (e.g. Jim, Joe and Mary), there are many different species of *Coprosma* (e.g. *Coprosma acerosa, Coprosma repens, Coprosma robusta*, etc.). It is annoying at a family gathering of Smiths to keep repeating everyone's surname, and botanical naming copes with this problem by abbreviating the generic name to its initial capital letter after first mention (e.g. *C. acerosa, C. repens, C. robusta*). The abbreviation for 'species' is 'spp.', i.e. *Sophora* spp. refers to the different species of *Sophora*.

Interspecific hybrids (i.e. crosses between two different species) are written with a multiplication sign between the generic and specific epithets (e.g. *Coprosma* ×*kirkii*, which is a hybrid between *Coprosma acerosa* and *Coprosma repens*). Cultivars are selected from species or hybrids through artificial selection, and their names are covered separately by the International Code of Nomenclature for Cultivated Plants. Cultivar names follow the botanical names and are never italicised or underlined; they always begin with a capital letter and are enclosed by single apostrophes (e.g. *Coprosma* ×*kirkii* 'Kirkii'). The cultivar 'Kirkii' is a seedling selection from the hybrid cross and is thereafter maintained in cultivation by vegetatively propagated cuttings. Botanical varieties arise naturally and are minor morphological variations of a species. Because people are not involved in their selection and development, as they are with cultivars, naming of botanical varieties are covered by the rules of the International Code of Botanical Nomenclature. The abbreviation var. is used to indicate a botanical variety, for example *Celmisia semicordata* var. *stricta*.

A synonym, abbreviated to syn., following a name, for example *Brachyglottis* syn. *Senecio*, indicates that the first name is the new name (*Brachyglottis*) for an old generic name (*Senecio*). Both names refer to the same plant.

# Designing your garden

At the end of the design process your garden should be functional, low maintenance and aesthetically pleasing. Design is about solving problems. In a garden, the placement of paths, drives and vistas is important, but equally important are those other issues that can affect the functionality of the design; for example, ensuring that your budget is adequate and that the plants chosen are capable of growing well in your area.

The ability to minimise potential problems relating to future plant growth may also be important. Avoid planting plants such as flax (*Phormium*) too close to paths or access ways. Because of the habit of growth of flax, they grow as an ever-widening clump, after a few years, long, lax leaves can become a tripping hazard. If the budget or time for maintenance is limited, planting ground cover plants that grow larger will make it easier for them to compete with potential weeds, and most of the smaller annual weeds can be easily out-competed.

For specialist advice on garden design, it is usually worth consulting a qualified landscape architect.

Left: Ground cover used with other New Zealand native species in a more formal setting: *Hebe* (border plants in front), *Scleranthus* (the very low carpet former, middle front), *Pachystegia* (middle rear), *Griselinia* (hedge, rear, including taller *Podocarpus* species).

Above: Strong lines and textural elements are displayed in this setting by the use of clump formers: *Carex* (front), *Anemanthele* (next) and *Phormium*. At the rear are *Hebe* and *Cordyline* species.

Right: A mixture of line and textural elements, spreaders and clump formers: *Arthropodium* (front), *Brachyglottis* (middle left) and *Hebe* (middle right); at the back are *Pachystegia*, with *Austroderia richardii* (toetoe) behind, *Coprosma* (middle) and the pale-leaved *Ozothamnus* at right.

## Colour, line, form and texture

When selecting ground cover, the leaf characteristics are generally more important than the qualities of the flowers and fruits. For most species, flowers and fruits are only seen for a relatively short period of time. There are some exceptions to this; for example, the flowers of some cultivars of *Hebe, Brachyglottis, Leptospermum* (mānuka) and the like are conspicuous for long periods.

When making these selections, think of the erect, striking lines that plants with large, linear leaves such as flax (*Phormium*) or *Astelia* have and the impact a few (or many) of these sorts of plants will have on the final outcome of the garden. Compare them to the smaller-leaved prostrate-growing plants such as *Pimelea*. Think of large leaves, such as Chatham Island forget-me-not (*Myosotidium hortensia*), versus small-leaved plants, such as whipcord hebes (*Hebe armstrongii, Leonohebe cupressoides*, etc.). The difference in leaf size provides the textural element. Plants can be categorised as fine textured (small leaves), medium textured (middle-sized leaves) or coarse (large leaves).

Equally important when thinking about New Zealand native ground cover plants are the foliage colours. New Zealand plants exhibit a remarkable range of coloured foliage, in a wide variety of greens, browns, yellows, purples, and grey to blue shades. The different colours can be used to good effect in any garden, and as most New Zealand native plants are evergreen the effect created lasts all year round.

Finally, as we have seen, there is a wide range of plant forms, from prostrate creeping plants to bun-shaped plants, to plants that have divaricating forms that often have a sprawling habit, or those that form clumps.

## Calculating how many plants you will need

By planning ahead, you will have time to prepare the ground for planting, and you can determine the best way to propagate or obtain your plants, or whether to contract someone to grow them for you. Otherwise the large numbers of plants you may want may not be available when you are ready for them.

Before you can calculate the number of each type of plant you require, you will need to have gone through the design process. Once this is done it is easy enough to measure the areas involved and divide them by the likely spread of each individual plant. The ultimate size of an individual plant will be an estimate, because plants continue to grow and given unrestricted space may grow much larger than the space you allot to them. The closer you site each plant in relation to another, the faster the plants will cover the ground and generally the more uniform the cover will be. When the ground has been covered by the plants, growth is limited by the reduced potential for each plant to occupy any more space for increased light interception, and reduced space for roots to extract water and nutrients from the soil.

Native ground cover plants offer a wide range of coloured foliage (left to right): *Brachyglottis* 'Crustii', *Rubus* X *barkeri*, *Phormium* 'Sunset', *Libertia peregrinans*, *Geranium sessiliflorum* 'Purpureum', *Acaena caesiiglauca.*

Once you have made an estimate of how much space each species of plant should have, use the following formula to calculate how many plants you will need.

---

**Calculating the number of plants**

Use the formula: $\dfrac{\text{area in square metres}}{(\text{distance between plants})^2}$

For example, assume a particular plant might eventually spread to cover 0.8 m x 0.8 m and you have an area to plant of 3 m x 5 m (15 square metres, or 15 m²). If we enter these figures into the formula we get:

$$\frac{15\,m^2}{(0.8)^2} = \frac{15}{0.64} = \text{24 plants required.}$$

For a plant requiring 0.4 m x 0.4 m, and assuming the same-sized area of 3 m x 5 m, we get:

$$\frac{15\,m^2}{(0.4)^2} = \frac{15}{0.16} = \text{94 plants required.}$$

Using the formula above, the number of plants required for any size area can be calculated.

---

## The best height for ground cover plants

Although we suggested earlier that ground cover plants may be any species of virtually any size, in a small garden people will often tend to think of low-growing plants as being the most suitable. However, it is important to be aware that some very low-growing plants soon become an ideal nursery for slightly larger and then larger again weeds to become established. There are certain instances where the use of tiny ground-hugging plants may actually come to involve very high maintenance, in terms of continuously needing weeding.

For large areas that are to be planted out with ground cover, it may be better to choose taller-growing plants so as to reduce potential weed problems. In larger gardens, where you do not have a lot of time for weeding ground covers, choose species that grow at least 30 cm in height. In very small gardens, growing ground cover plants that are just a few centimetres high will involve considerable weeding, but they are less likely to become a maintenance nightmare.

# Propagating New Zealand native ground cover plants

## Choosing your propagation method

Depending on the scale of the garden being planted, ground cover plants may be required in large quantities. Purchasing these from garden centres may work out to be very expensive, and with a little effort you may be able to grow them yourself, in advance of planting.

Most species of plants can be propagated by seed, spores or vegetative means. Seeds usually produce some variability, and while most plants grown from seed may look the same, some might be larger or smaller, others might be more or less susceptible to pests and diseases, or to temperature variation, and so on. Plants grown by vegetative means, such as by cuttings or division, are usually uniform in terms of appearance and vigour because they are clones of the parent plant.

Left: Stem cuttings of assorted New Zealand native plant species.

## Seeds and spores

Seeds and spores are the products of the reproductive phases in the life cycles of plants. As horticulturists we are mostly involved with seeds, because seed plants make up the largest and most diverse group in the plant kingdom. Interest in sowing spores is usually confined to those growing ferns and fern allies. Plants such as mosses and liverworts also reproduce by spores, but few of us are likely to be interested in propagating them: they will arrive, invited or not, if the conditions are suitable.

## Growing plants by seed or by vegetative methods

Propagation by seed is a good way to grow many New Zealand native plants, especially where the aim is re-vegetation, where maximum species diversity is desirable. Re-vegetation is about trying to reproduce the native plant community that was once growing in a particular location. Because each plant grown from seed can be slightly different, even within a species, nature has built in the ability for some plants to be able to survive in conditions where the majority might not. This variability ultimately allows for species to respond to changes in the environment and helps the species to survive.

In a garden, however, where plant uniformity is often a requirement, certain plants may be better propagated by vegetative means. Plants may have been selected from a variable species in the wild for certain 'desirable' characteristics, or distinguishing features. These sorts of characteristics may be a different leaf colour, or a plant with a more compact form, or possibly a plant with better flowering qualities than is normal for the species. Such plant selections have often been given cultivar names, and some of them may be protected by plant variety rights (PVR), which are like patents for new plant cultivars. More generally, plants may be propagated vegetatively because it is a more convenient way to produce plants of a particular species than by seed.

## Suiting the environment: provenance and hybrids

Provenance is the term used to refer to the geographic location and environmental conditions from which seeds or plants are collected. Provenance may have a strong impact on the subsequent growth of plants in an entirely different location. For instance, when grown in cooler areas, plants from warmer areas may not include genes for hardiness. In other words, the performance of plants grown from seed may be strongly linked to the area or conditions from where they were originally sourced.

Seed may also be of variable quality depending on where it was originally sourced, and may either be genetically diverse or produce seedlings true to type. If you want to grow plants in any extreme environment it would be wise to obtain seed with a provenance that experiences those same conditions – locally, if possible.

Hybrids are important in the production of many garden plants. They may arise by chance or by deliberate attempts to create something new and distinct from what already exists. Where two species of the same genus meet in the wild, there is often a population exhibiting intermediate forms (hybrids) between the two species. There are many examples of interspecific hybrids that have occurred naturally in New Zealand's flora. Some of the most obvious are found in the genera *Hebe, Corokia* and *Coprosma*. Selections made from hybrid crosses, whether occurring naturally or created deliberately through cross-pollination, are known as cultivars and are propagated vegetatively to increase and maintain the new plants in cultivation.

## Propagating by seed

Many New Zealand native species flower over the spring and into early summer. Seed is often best collected in autumn or early winter, soon after ripening, although the best times for collecting seeds may vary slightly between species. Seeds are contained within the 'fruit' (botanically speaking) of the ripened ovary of a flower. This may contain accessory floral or vegetative tissue in the case of angiosperms (flowering plants), or the seed may be attached to a scale in some type of cone, as in gymnosperms (mostly conifers). Ferns reproduce by spores, which can be collected by removing some of the fronds (leaves) with sporangia (spore cases) containing the spores.

Alternatively, garden centres supply and sell seeds, and botanical and horticultural organisations will supply (and may give away) seeds to their members.

*Asplenium bulbiferum* showing spore cases.

## Extracting seed

Seeds will often need to be extracted from the fruit. There are many different types of seeds and fruits, which will influence seed extraction methods. Fleshy fruits (berries) containing seeds, such as in *Astelia*, *Coprosma*, *Fuchsia* and *Lobelia,* can be placed in sieves and put in a sink under running water until the flesh of the berry gradually washes away. Sometimes, soaking the fruit in still, shallow water for a day or two before running them under a tap helps break down the fleshy tissue before washing it off. The washing of flesh from seeds can also help remove material that inhibits germination in some seeds (an *inhibitor*; see below under 'Seed dormancy'). Once seed has been separated completely from the flesh, it can be sown, or stored dry in a labelled jar in a fridge.

Seeds in dry capsules or pods, such as found on kōwhai (*Sophora*), flax (*Phormium*) and New Zealand iris (*Libertia*), can be separated by crushing the fruit between two surfaces and blowing away the chaff. Ideally, some sort of shallow-sided box and something like as a wooden concreting float or an old wooden rolling pin can be used to gently crush the dried fruit. It may be helpful to line the base of the box and the wooden float with corrugated rubber matting lining. Seed from plants such as mānuka (*Leptospermum scoparium*) and kānuka (*Kunzea ericoides*) can be obtained by putting the capsules into a container; the seed is released as the capsules dry out over time. Note that some seeds in capsules, such as *Pittosporum tenuifolium* (kōhūhū), are very sticky. Adding some very fine sand or talcum powder can help to separate them.

Seeds in dry capsules or pods (left to right): *Leptospermum scoparium, Pittosporum tenuifolium, Hebe speciosa, Phormium tenax.*

*Polystichum vestitum* showing spore cases (sori).

Fern spores can be collected by placing sheets of paper below the fertile fronds of a fern, shaking the fronds and then carefully tipping the spores into an envelope. Another method is to tie paper bags around a portion of a frond containing spores. Fern spores need a shady, moist area for germination. The fern life cycle is fundamentally different to that of seed plants. Ferns have two distinct growth stages. The first is a tiny, almost invisible, plant, which has separate male and female sex organs that produce male and female gametes. These combine when the male gamete swims through water to fuse with the female gamete, thus producing the true fern plant. The true fern is better adapted to growing in drier sites than is the first stage.

## Seed storage

The ability of a seed to germinate (viability) reduces with the passing of time. In some species seeds are short lived and should be sown soon after harvest. Species with long-lived seeds may have hard seed coat dormancy (see below) and their seeds may be impervious to water. Other seeds can be stored for long periods of time if dried to less than 10% moisture and given appropriate storage conditions.

Providing appropriate storage conditions for seed will help maintain germination rates for longer. Some seeds cannot be dried and stored because they lose their viability as they dry out. Seeds from this group are normally sown soon after ripening, or are stored for no more than a few months in moist peat or sphagnum moss, often after dusting with a fungicide. Examples include the larger seeds, such as those of karaka (*Corynocarpus laevigatus*) and mountain tōtara (*Podocarpus nivalis*). Generally, seed can be stored for a year or so at low temperatures, usually between about 2 and 4°C, in a fridge. Seed stored in warmer conditions, in areas of high humidity or in the sun will not last as well.

## Seed dormancy

There are two main types of seed dormancy that can prevent germination. The first of these is 'seed coat dormancy'. Species with long-lived seed may have a hard seed coat that is impervious to water. The impervious seed coat inhibits water uptake and gas exchange, provides a mechanical barrier that stops the embryo expanding, prevents leaching of growth inhibitors, such as abscisic acid, from the embryo, and may even produce growth inhibitors.

Fully ripened seeds extracted from pods tend to have hard seed coat dormancy, such as kōwhai (*Sophora*). These need to have the seed coat chipped or acid treated (i.e. scarified) to allow water to be taken up by the seed before germination can occur. By soaking seeds in concentrated sulphuric acid (e.g. soak kōwhai seeds for 30 minutes and then carefully decant off the acid into water to safely dilute the acid before washing any remaining acid from the seeds), many seeds can be easily scarified. (Some growers might collect the seed before it is fully mature and the seed coat is still soft and thus avoid the need to scarify the seed.)

Other methods can be used for a small quantity of seeds, such as cutting each seed coat with a sharp knife or rumbling the seeds in a rotating tumbler containing a coarse grade of sharp sand. Hot-water soaks have been suggested, but care is needed to ensure the water is not so hot that the seed embryo is killed. For most home gardeners, carefully chipping off a thin piece of seed coat with a sharp knife is the best option.

The other type of dormancy is 'embryo dormancy'. This is where the seed exerts some form of internal control by means of a growth inhibitor (e.g. abscisic acid), which prevents seeds from germinating. In the natural environment the inhibitor prevents the seed from germinating too early, before the worst of the winter weather is over, so that young seedlings do not perish in the extreme winter months.

Often moist, cool chilling (stratification) of seeds is all that is needed to break this form of dormancy. To speed this process up in a nursery situation, seeds can be stratified by placing them in moist sand or sphagnum moss in a fridge between 0 and 2°C for up to three months before sowing. For some species, applying gibberellic acid (a growth promoter) to the seed has been shown to overcome the need for stratification and to improve germination.

## Sowing seeds

Seeds can be sown in pots or trays and germinated in greenhouses, or sown directly outside. A piece of chicken wire to cover the seeds will stop birds from eating seedlings after germination. To maintain some control of outdoor sowing it is a good idea to sow in rows in soil prepared as you would for a vegetable garden. However, do not add any fertiliser to the ground when you sow seed.

If you are sowing seeds into containers it is best to purchase a proprietary seed mix. These are normally soil-less media and have a very low level of fertilisers, often just a small amount of superphosphate to promote root growth, plus lime to correct the pH of the medium.

Seeds should be sown thinly and evenly in the tray, or in a row outside, and then covered with a fine layer of whatever medium you are using.

In both the garden row outside and in the pot or tray, the medium should be firmed after the seeds have been covered. A wooden concreting float is a good option for firming media in trays. The back of a rake pressed down on the ground after covering the seed with soil is ideal for the garden row. Consolidating the medium after sowing provides the seed with intimate contact with the soil or soil-less medium. This reduces the aeration around the seed but improves contact with soil moisture. As plants germinate and grow in the ground outside, or are re-potted, the aeration rate will return to normal.

Germination relies on three key factors: viable seed, a suitable environment in which to germinate (adequate water and air, and correct temperature and light or dark conditions) and the absence of any seed dormancy controls. Generally, temperatures of about 12 to 15°C will be optimal for most seeds to germinate, providing other preconditions have been met. Temperature requirements may vary between species, and the range for each species may be specific or broad. Some seeds germinate best with an even temperature, while others germinate better with fluctuating temperatures. In some species seed may require specific periods of dark or light conditions before germination occurs. The time seeds take to germinate will vary depending on both the environmental conditions provided and the species.

Damping-off diseases can be problematic, especially if seeds are sown too thickly or the soil or medium is infected. The main culprits are either fungi or water moulds, with spores that can be spread in water. Symptoms of damping off include girdled stems and root rot of seedlings, visible as circular dead patches of seedlings within a tray. Both post- and pre-emergence rots may be involved. Ways of helping to prevent damping-off diseases include sowing seeds at a lower density, using soil-less seed-raising media and fungicides, and ensuring that surroundings and containers are clean, the temperature is appropriate, and that water drains well.

'Pricking out' refers to the transplanting of young germinated seedlings into larger containers with more space for the young plants to establish. Seedlings are handled by gently loosening the medium around the roots, often using a dibber (a piece of wood the size and shape of a pencil). This is pushed through the medium below the seedlings and levered upwards, loosening the roots and the medium in the process. Then the young seedling is gently lifted by holding the cotyledons (seed leaves) and transplanting it to another container for 'growing on'. The same dibber can be used to create a hole for the roots of the seedling being transplanted. After the new container is full with newly planted seedlings, it is important to water these in carefully before any drying out can occur.

If seedlings are to be grown on in containers, make sure you purchase a good potting mix. This will contain slow-release fertilisers that will help maintain plant growth.

## Propagation by vegetative means

There are a number of common methods used to propagate plants by vegetative means. By using these methods the plant you produce is likely to be the same as the parent you obtained the plant material from. Some New Zealand native plants are dioecious (have separate male and female plants), so if you specifically want either the male or female plant then the only certain way of achieving this is by vegetative propagation. The female plant is the one that produces the fruit (e.g. berries). You cannot be certain whether you have male or female plants by growing them from seed until they flower, and that can take many years for some species.

Another reason for using vegetative methods of propagation is if you want to grow a plant with known characteristics. These could be plants with a particular selected form that differs from the normal seed-grown plants: it may grow to a particular size, or it may have particular flower or fruiting qualities that are desirable.

The most common method of propagation in plant nurseries is by cuttings or division. To a lesser degree layering, budding and grafting techniques can be used. In some specialist nurseries, plants are started by tissue culture and often sold to other nurseries for growing on.

## Division of clumps

In the home garden, certain types of ground cover can be multiplied quite easily depending on their mode of growth. Plants that grow as ever-widening clumps, such as flax (*Phormium*), and others such as *Astelia*, *Uncinia*, *Carex* and some *Libertia* spp., can be dug up and divided during the cooler months between autumn and mid-spring. It is easy to tease apart the younger plants and roots that are found on the outer part of the clump. Provided the roots are not allowed to dry out at any stage, many new plants can be produced by dividing a single clump.

A single clump of *Phormium* 'Jester' divided up into five separate plants and lined out to grow larger before planting each into its final position in the garden.

## Layering

Many plants that carpet the ground by growing more or less flat often produce new roots toward the outer margins where the branch tips make contact with the ground. This is a form of natural layering. Plant portions with roots can be cut from the parent plant, carefully dug out and replanted, producing many more plants. Plants in this group include *Acaena*, some *Hebe* spp. and cultivars, *Parahebe*, *Heliohebe*, and some of the prostrate *Coprosma* spp.

Layering can also be used to encourage roots to form on stems or branches when they would not normally do so. The simplest way is to bend a branch down so that it comes into contact with the soil surface. The lower side of the branch can be cut with a sharp knife at the point of contact with the soil and rooting hormone powder applied, and the branch pegged to maintain intimate contact with the soil surface. The cut area encourages a build-up of carbohydrates, and the stem when subjected to moisture and dark provides conditions likely to encourage new roots to form.

Essentially, a layer is like a cutting with insurance. The insurance is that it still receives water and carbohydrates from the parent plant, whereas a cutting, once removed from the parent plant, loses that support and can dry out and die very quickly. Layering is not used so much in commercial nurseries today, but it can be a satisfactory method for home gardeners to try, without the need for any sophisticated equipment. Expect the rooted layers to take anything up to a year to develop, but in some easy-to-root species it can be just a matter of weeks, depending on the time of year.

## Rhizomes

The third major vegetative method is to propagate from those plants that spread by rhizomes (underground stems). These plants can be cut and dug up with a portion of rhizome with roots attached. Examples of species with this characteristic include ferns such as *Blechnum pennamarina*, and flowering species such as *Arthropodium cirratum* and *Fuchsia procumbens*. The best time to propagate plants in this manner is during autumn, winter or spring.

## Cuttings

Growing plants by cuttings is the main means of vegetative plant propagation used by plant nurseries, and it is worth describing here in some detail.

## Stem cuttings

The majority of trees, shrubs and sub-shrubs are grown by stem cuttings. Stem cuttings require some stem material, nodes with axillary buds, and a few leaves. The buds in the axils of the leaves are necessary to produce new shoots. Roots are initiated from the stem base area. Stem cuttings are described as either softwood, semi-ripe or hardwood. This classification is broadly based on the ripeness of the stem, or, in other words, the degree of woodiness in the stem.

New growth in a stem in spring is soft. As it begins to develop lignin the stem begins to firm, and finally at the end of summer the wood is fully ripened. Generally, as the lignification process proceeds the ability of the cutting to produce roots lessens. In some easy-to-root species this may have no obvious effects, but for most plants the optimal time to take cuttings will depend on the species involved. For many New Zealand trees and shrubs, mid-summer to late autumn are good times to take cuttings. For some that are harder to strike, semi-ripe cuttings give better results. For plant material that is very difficult to strike, plant propagators may prefer to use softwood cuttings taken in spring, but they need to ensure they are protected with fungicides because this type of cutting is prone to rot.

Cuttings should be taken in the cool of the day and prevented from drying out until they are prepared and set in the appropriate rooting medium. Once set, cuttings should not be allowed to dry out at any stage. Cuttings are described as nodal or internodal, although generally it does not seem to matter which type is made. The node is the position on the stem where the leaf arises. An internodal cutting is one where the base of the cutting is roughly midway between the two nodes, and a nodal cutting is cut immediately below the node.

The length of cuttings will depend on the amount of material available for propagation, the ease of propagation for that species, and the type of facilities available to the propagator. If you have access to base heat and overhead misting systems in a propagating house, small cuttings can be made and easily maintained. Sometimes much larger cuttings may be necessary, but for most purposes cuttings between 100 and 150 mm in length are sufficient.

Cuttings should usually be made from lateral shoot growth, not have any flowers or fruits, and be free from pests and diseases. Cuttings that have poor health usually take longer to propagate and often produce unthrifty plants. Plant material that appears to be growing vigorously often has very high levels of nitrogen, and high nitrogen levels in cuttings have been shown to inhibit root development. These cuttings are often more susceptible to fungal attacks in the propagation stage.

In preparing the cuttings, remove the lower leaves so that the lower 30 to 50 mm of stem is clean, which allows the cuttings to be more easily set in the rooting medium. Some cuttings may benefit from applying rooting hormone. Commercial products containing the rooting hormone IBA (indole-3-butyric acid) can be purchased from garden centres.

Some cuttings also benefit from being 'wounded'. This normally means taking a thin sliver of bark from one or both sides of the lower 5 to 10 mm on the base of the cutting. This has been shown to improve the uptake of water and provides a greater surface area for the uptake of rooting hormones, thus stimulating root formation.

## Leaf cuttings and plantlets

Some New Zealand native plants can be grown by leaf cuttings, including succulents such as horokaka or New Zealand iceplant (*Disphyma australe*). Other plants such as the hen and chicken fern (*Asplenium bulbiferum*) produce plantlets on their fronds; when mature, these plantlets drop onto the ground and rapidly produce roots. The plantlets are clones of the parent plant. In a garden or nursery these plantlets can be taken from the fronds and potted up.

The succulent-leaved
*Disphyma australe*.

## Procedure for setting cuttings

The rooting medium has to meet the following criteria:

- clean and weed free
- low nutrient status (a rooting medium rarely has any added nutrients)
- able to support the cuttings once inserted
- free draining
- well aerated.

Different propagators will often have their own favourite rooting medium, but each recipe will usually meet the above criteria. Medium to coarse pumice or medium to coarse washed river sand are both good media. Sometimes they may be mixed with organic material such as peat or sphagnum moss. Where base heat and misting systems are available, sciarid fly can thrive and its larvae attack the new roots of growing cuttings. Sciarid fly particularly thrive where organic materials such as peat are used in the propagating media. By using pumice, perlite or sand without any organic material you can help prevent this pest establishing.

Clean plastic trays or pots with good drainage holes in the base can be used to grow the cuttings in. It is a good idea to label the cuttings and put the date when they were taken.

Once the cuttings have been set they need to be carefully watered in and placed either somewhere cool, such as a shade house or on the shady side of your house, or, if you have better facilities, on a base heat of 15 to 20°C. In conjunction with this it is usual to have some sort of misting system. This can operate either on a time clock or on an electronic leaf (a device that regulates overhead misting). Both of these control the amount of mist provided to cool the leaves of the cuttings and prevent water loss through transpiration. Ideally, more mist is supplied to the plants during the warmer periods and misting is reduced during colder periods. It is important that cuttings remain moist until they have developed their own roots.

Once the cuttings have developed sufficient roots to be safely removed from the propagating medium, they can be potted up into potting mix, or planted in a part of the garden that can be used to safely grow on the plants. A good root system on a typical-size cutting could be a mass of roots about the size of a golf ball. If you only have a few thick roots, as is typical when using firmly packed river sand, the rooting medium might have had poor aeration. Sometimes cuttings with poor root systems, if they have taken a long time to get to that point, can still be carefully shifted into the garden or potting mix.

Probably the worst thing a plant propagator can do is continuously lift cuttings to see if they have produced roots. Be patient: often it is better to wait for signs of roots emerging from the base of the container before transplanting. If you have hundreds of cuttings, lifting a few to check progress occasionally will not matter.

## Potting up or planting out rooted cuttings

Having some good, clean, weed-free garden space is useful for lining out newly rooted cuttings. Growing them on in containers before planting out is another option. If the cuttings have been grown outside, then the former option is the best one. If they have been grown under warm greenhouse conditions, then the plants may be better grown in larger containers in a sheltered area for a time so that the plants can be gradually hardened off to acclimatise to outdoor conditions.

In the garden situation, plants can be lined out in clear ground (such as the vegetable garden), spacing each plant about 150 mm apart in a row. These can then be grown on, weeded and watered as necessary until the autumn, when they can be transplanted into their appropriate setting in the garden. Generally there is no need to add fertilisers to improve growth rates in the soil during this stage.

If you decide to pot up your rooted cuttings, the simplest way is to purchase a good-quality potting mix. Depending on how long you need to grow the plants in a pot, you can buy mixes with slow-release fertilisers based on the anticipated needs. Potting mixes are manufactured with between 3 and 18 months' supply of nutrients. Modern potting mixes are generally peat or crushed bark, with lime added to bring the pH up to an acceptable level, plus slow-release fertilisers containing both macro- and micro-nutrients. Ideally, plants should not be kept in pots for too long, as one of the major problems for potted plants is roots encircling each other inside the pot.

Plants can be grown in pots with garden soil. Here the main problem will be weed growth, as soil generally contains weed seeds and these will need to be removed as they germinate, before the weeds establish. Plants grown in soil are generally better buffered against drying out than plants in soil-less media and soil is much heavier and more stable, which means the pots are less likely to be blown over outside in windy conditions. Plants grown in potting mix will grow well, but extra care is needed to ensure plants are regularly watered. However, garden soil in pots is not as well aerated and usually stays wetter than most soil-less potting mixes, leading to unsatisfactory growth. (The air porosity ratio of a soil or potting mix depends on the physical particle size of the media used. Larger particle sizes mixed together produce larger pores; conversely, small particle sizes produce small pores. These pores can be filled with air or water and change as drainage occurs. Garden soils have finer particle sizes, and therefore less pore space, than potting mixes of peat or bark, and as a result are wetter and not as well aerated.)

If you are growing lots of plants in containers and require consistency, a good soil-less medium is likely to have better drainage and air-filled porosity, providing more uniform growth. Plants grown in soil-less media do require more careful management and more frequent watering, but they are less likely to require weeding than soil-based potted plants. Another option is to thoroughly mix garden soil and potting mix in equal parts, pot up your plants in containers, and then apply straight potting mix for the top 4 to 5 cm to prevent weed growth. If you do this, you need to be aware that the top of the container will often appear dry, even though significant moisture is held in the lower parts of the container.

## Placement of container-grown plants

If you are planning on growing a large number of plants and putting them into containers, it might be worth placing them on some form of wire mesh suspended on blocks about 15 cm above the ground. The purpose of this is to prevent roots growing through the drainage holes in the base of the container and into the ground below. If roots do grow into the ground below, separating pots from soil and roots can be difficult, and sometimes if plants are wrenched from the ground they may die.

Another advantage of sitting plants in containers on wire mesh above the ground is that new roots that emerge from the base of the container are effectively air pruned and this controls the rate of growth of the top of the plant. This means that plants can be left growing for longer in pots than might otherwise be possible. Nursery growers will often grow plants in root trainers, which prevent roots from circling within the pot. Root trainers and similar containers have holes in the sides and base, and often have vertical ribs inside the container, which prevent roots circling and allow greater air pruning of the root system.

## Planting out established plants

### Planting out from the open ground

If you are shifting plants from the open ground that have been lined out earlier, make sure you *wrench* the plants first. Wrenching involves cutting the roots of the plants that are to be shifted a few weeks in advance of lifting and shifting. A simple method for the home gardener is to use a spade to cut the roots around the plant. For plants in a row, just cut the sides of the roots along both sides of the row, again using a spade. Make the cut more or less vertically, normally at the edge of where the foliage stops. If the plants are well established in the ground (having been there for a year or more), more time and preparation

before moving them may be required. Some adjustment to where you wrench the plants may be required if the plants are especially large, as the weight of the soil to be carried will need to be considered. For larger trees the diameter of the rootball is generally 10 to 12 times the trunk diameter at about 1.5 m above ground level.

It may pay to get advice, as some plants such as celmisias and mānuka (*Leptospermum scoparium*) do not transplant very easily. In general, shifting plants from open ground is best done from late autumn until the end of winter, when growth has slowed. Some plants may require support staking, depending on their size, and some may require some pruning of their shoots, depending on how much root loss has occurred. (If in doubt, ask for a horticulturist's advice.)

*Leptospermum scoparium* 'Red Falls'.

## Planting out from containers

This sounds simple enough, and generally it is, but there are a few considerations that may help overcome some potential problems.

### Planting times

Plants can be planted out from containers all year round. However, if you intend planting during the summer you will need to be much more vigilant to ensure newly planted plants do not dry out before they become established. Ideally, planting should take place during the autumn to mid-spring. In this way you greatly increase the likelihood of plants establishing.

### Soil and potting mix

Most plants from commercial nurseries are produced in light-weight, free-draining potting mixes. Soil is generally heavier and does not drain as quickly. When planting from containers, carefully place the potting mix and roots into the hole, then add some soil around the surface and gently firm it in. Make sure the plant is watered well. In theory the job is done and you can go away and forget about that plant for a while.

In practice, the water that goes into the potting mix at the base of the plant is soon drained into the surrounding soil, where none of the plant's roots have yet had time to grow. The smaller particles of the soil also have a stronger attraction for the water through capillary movement than the coarser particles of most potting mixes, so a plant that you think has been well watered may soon dry out. It is important to break up the roots of a plant in potting mix very carefully and mix the soil and potting mix at the base of the hole to try to minimise the potential for rapid drying out around the roots. For the same reason, adding organic material at planting without thoroughly mixing it with the soil can create problems with water movement.

The addition of fertiliser in the planting hole is generally not necessary. If used at all, only add small amounts of slow-release fertilisers well mixed in with the soil. This can be beneficial.

## Planting depth and staking

For the majority of plants, planting at the same depth as they were before (either in the open ground or in a container) is sensible. In very light, well-drained soils, such as sandy or shingle soils, it is probably better to plant a bit deeper. For heavy, wet soils, such as some with high amounts of clay, it may be best to plant slightly proud of (above) the previous planting depth.

In rare cases, staking may be necessary, but this should be a last resort. It is generally better to plant small, hardy plants in groups. Smaller plants are able to establish better than large plants because they are less likely to have their root systems rocked around by wind. Plants with large tops and relatively small roots at planting time will need staking to anchor the root system.

If you are growing plants such as these, it is important to stake them carefully so that the stakes and ties do not themselves cause future damage to the plant. The worst damage occurs when a tree is tied to a single stake in a way that does not allow the trunk to flex normally. A tree tied between two or three stakes at just one point low to the ground, is generally the best option. Damage from staking too rigidly usually occurs when ties cut into the soft wood of the trunk, the trunk rubs against the stake, or trees are left staked for too long. Normally, stakes are only required for one growing season, or at most two, before they are removed. Observations show that with trees that are staked for longer than this, the root system is often smaller than it would be if it had not been staked and the top of the tree is larger, both ultimately working against the tree's likelihood of future survival.

# Ground preparation: weeds, cultivation and herbicides

## The battle against weeds

Integral to good ground preparation is the idea that all weeds, especially perennial weeds, should be eradicated before planting out ground cover plants. However, even if this is achieved, further weed seeds will germinate and other weeds will arrive in your garden without invitation. A totally weed-free garden is an illusion, and the battle for a maintenance-free garden, even with ground cover plants, requires an awareness of what is likely to occur and having a sound strategy to deal with it. If you are prepared for this and learn how to deal with weeds, you are well on the way to having a successful low-maintenance garden.

A good book on weeds with lots of colour plates would be a useful addition to your library, such as *An Illustrated Guide to Common Weeds of New Zealand* (see Popay et al. under Useful references at the back of this book).

Left: *Leptinella squalida.*

## Types of weeds

Weeds are variously described by different authors, but one of the most common definitions of a weed is a plant that is growing in a place where it is not wanted. Another perspective is that nature knows no plants as weeds, or that weeds are simply plants whose virtues have not yet been discovered. There are some that see any exotic plants (plants that have been introduced from other countries) that are capable of naturalising (able to produce seed and grow in their new environment without help from people) in New Zealand as weeds. There are many other definitions, but generally weeds are unwanted plants that grow where we do not want them. In some instances, a weed to one person will be a garden treasure to another.

Weeds are broadly of two main types: those that spread mainly by seed and those that reproduce by some vegetative means. The latter are typically the most difficult to eradicate. Some weeds have the ability to both seed freely and reproduce by vegetative means, and they can become very invasive. Blackberry (*Rubus fruticosus*) is one such example.

Weeds that seed freely have a number of modifications to help them spread around the countryside. Some weed species have fleshy fruit that encourages animals and birds to eat the fruit and distribute the seeds – with a dollop of fresh organic fertiliser to help get things started. Often in the process the seed coat is acid treated by the stomach contents. This natural acid treatment scarifies the seed coat and is often a prerequisite for germination to occur.

Members of the daisy family (Asteraceae) have modified sepals that act like a parachute in the wind (e.g. dandelion seeds). Other seeds float in water and spread along drains and streams, while some have hooks or claws for attaching themselves to animals or to people's clothing. Animals such as cats can introduce or continue to bring clinging seeds such as cleavers (*Galium aparine*) from neglected gardens nearby.

Buying in soil or organic compost is another way in which the unwitting gardener is likely to introduce a range of new weed species into a garden. Be especially cautious of receiving plant material with soil on its roots from well-meaning friends. For example, look out for rhizomatous weeds such as twitch (*Elytrigia repens*) and convolvulus (*Calystegia silvatica*) growing through the roots of desirable plants dug from other gardens and gifted to you.

Some seeds can lie dormant in the soil for long periods. This issue of seed dormancy is very important. Plant species employ a number of survival strategies. One of these, very successfully employed by many weed species, is that after the seeds are shed, only some seeds germinate while others remain dormant and will not germinate until later. Some seeds may survive in the ground dormant for many years; gorse is a good example of this, but there are many other species like this.

As with seeds of ground cover plants, sometimes seed dormancy in weeds is related to how thick or hard the seed coat is. In other cases it may be related to a requirement for exposure to specific light or dark conditions, or some quantitative chilling or warming period that needs to be experienced before germination will occur. Seeds shed by the same plant in any season are often quite variable within this range of factors and will usually germinate at quite different times, even though the majority of seeds may appear to germinate at one time.

## Annuals versus perennials

Many of the plants that seed freely are annuals. These plants usually complete their life cycle within a calendar year, often in just a few weeks during the growing season. Most of the seeds germinate in the spring and plants complete their life cycle by mid-summer. Some, however, may not begin to germinate until autumn, and over-winter before taking off in early spring

Weeds such as bitter cress are particularly annoying, often over-wintering and thus seeming to go from flower to seed within a few days, often with a number of generations in a year. Others, such as chickweed, develop rapidly in winter, smothering the ground before growth occurs for other plants. Field pansies, cleavers, fathen, scarlet pimpernel, annual poa, bindweed, amaranthus, stinging nettles, nightshade, fumitory, groundsel and other annual weeds can all be locally troublesome.

The important thing with weeds that seed freely is to prevent new weeds from seeding if possible. The old adage of one year seeding equals seven years' weeding is worth remembering. So after planting, remove any new weeds as they appear, preferably before flowering, to limit the future seed bank as much as possible and in the long run reduce the time involved with weeding. The idea is that as the ground cover plants develop and spread, they eventually reduce the opportunities for weeds to compete for water, space and nutrients. Eventually, once the ground

Weeds will compete well with low-growing ground cover, as in this garden where mallow, henbit, spurge and other weeds compete with *Leptinella squalida*.

cover plants have completely covered the ground, there is very little opportunity for weeds to compete. In contrast, if this is not properly put into practice, gardening with ground cover plants can be a continuous battle against weeds.

You can limit the effect of some potentially problematic weeds by planting more vigorous and taller-growing ground cover plants rather than low-growing species. Low-growing and particularly troublesome weeds, such as bitter cress (*Cardamine* spp.), will compete vigorously with low-growing ground cover plants such as *Scleranthus* or *Leptinella*, but will soon disappear if taller and more vigorous species, such as *Hebe albicans* or *Hebe* ✕*franciscana*, are chosen instead.

The second major group of troublesome weeds is the perennials. These plants are often already in the garden and need to be eradicated before any ground cover planting begins. Perennial plants are those that live for three years or more. They may be woody plants (e.g. gorse, broom, pines, willows and so on) or, more commonly in gardens, are non-woody perennial plants (e.g. twitch, field bindweed, wireweed, etc.). Non-woody perennial herbs may be evergreen or die down for part of the year. If they die down for part of the year they are described as herbaceous perennials; if they remain evergreen, they tend to be called perennial herbs. Perennial weeds may spread by seed as well as having some other vegetative means to occupy soil and aerial space.

Weeds such as the dandelion group, which includes groundsel, hawkbit, catsear, hawksbeard and hieracium, are reasonably well-known, yellow-flowered invaders, which often arrive from the air, but there are many other weeds in the Asteraceae that are perhaps not as well-known and that also pose a threat. Examples are bone seed (*Chrysanthemoides monilifera*), a shrubby, South African daisy common on the Port Hills in Canterbury, and capeweed (*Arctotheca calendula*), which is also now seen in parts of Canterbury.

All of the thistles have the same characteristics as the dandelion group, but are usually prickly and have purple-coloured flowers. Many of these weeds, as well as being very efficient seed spreaders, also have tap roots or rhizomes. As many of you will know, hoeing the top off a dandelion simply means new leaves and flowers will develop from the subterranean tap root. Cutting the top off a Californian thistle will lead to a similar result, except that the Californian thistle also has underground stems that can produce even more plants nearby.

Many of the perennial weeds spread by rhizomes (underground stems), and every time you cut a rhizome you effectively double the number of plants. Some of these weeds are particularly difficult to eradicate by cultivation and may require applications of systemic herbicide (see below). Examples of such perennial weeds are twitch (*Elytrigia repens*), greater bindweed (*Calystegia silvatica*), field bindweed (*Convolvulus arvensis*), yarrow (*Achillea millefolium*), sheep's sorrel (*Rumex acetosella*) and bracken fern (*Pteridium aquilinum*).

There are also a number of cultivated garden plants that can effectively become weeds, such as browntop (*Agrostis capillaris*, a lawn grass), garden mint (*Mentha* spp.), soapwort (*Saponaria officinalis*), rose of Sharon (*Hypericum calycinum*) and bear's breeches (*Acanthus mollis*), among others. Weeds such as dock (*Rumex* spp.) can be difficult to deal with, both because of their deep tap roots and because they are capable of producing large amounts of seed if not removed in time. The greater bindweed, or convolvulus (*Calystegia silvatica*), is a difficult rhizomatous perennial that should be eradicated before planting.

Other weeds creep across the ground by stolons, and some layer themselves as they go (via flat, above-ground stems that often produce new roots at nodes where the stem makes contact with the ground). Examples are creeping buttercup (*Ranunculus repens*), which is found mainly in moist soil, and periwinkle (*Vinca major* and *V. minor*). Both species of periwinkle have been used as garden plants in the past, but are also seen as weeds of waste space. Periwinkles have long, trailing stems and shallow rhizomes that regenerate easily.

Some other pernicious weeds, such as oxalis (*Oxalis latifolia* and other species) and montbretia (*Crocosmia ×crocosmiiflora*), produce a large quantity of small bulbs or corms each year, so that even if you carefully remove the plants, a few bulbs are generally left behind.

ↄ⟩ ↄ⟩ ↄ⟩ ↄ⟩ ↄ⟩

The above represent only some of the weeds that can be problems in New Zealand gardens. Before planting any ground cover plants, we strongly advise you to destroy all existing weeds, but especially perennial weeds. This will provide optimal conditions for ground cover plants to establish and will minimise subsequent maintenance. The weed eradication process can be expected to take at least one growing season to be reasonably sure all remaining rhizomes, stolons and tap roots of perennial weeds are no longer alive. You could use this time to propagate the ground cover plants for planting out in autumn, after weed eradication has been dealt with over the previous spring and summer period.

Weeds in gardens can be eradicated in a number of ways. The most obvious is through cultivation, but the other main option is the use of herbicides.

## Cultivation

In a small area this can be achieved through digging or forking over the area to be planted. Make sure the soil is not too wet before you start: if the soil sticks to your footwear, it is too wet and may become compressed, damaging the soil structure. During the process of turning over the soil, green weeds, rhizomes, stolons, bulbs and tap roots can be physically brought to the surface and removed. The ground can be levelled or graded as required, and then left.

After a few weeks, when the day is fine and the soil is on the dry side, hoe out any new weeds that have appeared and look for evidence of re-growth from perennial material still in the ground. Remove the perennial portions of weeds discovered and leave the small germinated seedlings on the soil surface to die in the sun. Repeat this process from about October (mid-spring) through until the end of February and your ground will be in ideal condition to plant in March or April (early to mid-autumn).

In a larger area, a similar result can be achieved through ploughing, using grubbers, discs, rotovators or rotary hoeing, followed by harrowing to stir up the top 10 to 15 cm of the soil surface. This destroys germinating annual weeds through desiccation, and similarly dries out perennial weed tissue in the form of rhizomes over the hotter months of summer.

# Herbicides

## Types of herbicide

Herbicides are chemical formulations that when properly applied kill weeds. Some herbicides are *non-selective* and kill any plants they come into contact with. Because non-selective herbicides kill all plants – desirable ones as well as weeds – you need to be very careful applying these.

Other herbicides are described as *selective* herbicides. For example, there are herbicides that have been developed to selectively remove broadleaf weeds. These have been available for some considerable time for use in lawns and other turf applications, particularly for sports turf. Hormone-based herbicides such as 2,4-D, 2,4,5-T and MCPA are very effective at killing broadleaf weeds in lawns without harming grasses, and have been developed further to include newer generation herbicides. Mecoprop is one of those used to control broadleaf weeds in lawns. There are also herbicides that are specifically designed to kill grass species only and can be generally used among broadleaf species. Care is needed when applying hormone-based weed killers around sensitive plants. In the vegetable garden, potatoes, tomatoes and grapes are especially susceptible to damage. It is important to always read the labels on herbicides for information about sensitive plants.

The selective and non-selective herbicides described so far can also be categorised as contact or knock-down herbicides, or systemic herbicides, based on their mode of action. Contact or knock-down herbicides are designed to kill weeds on contact and are generally most effective on annual weeds. When contact herbicides are used on perennial weeds, often they just kill the top green portion and then the weed regenerates from below-ground storage rhizomes or other parts of the plant. Systemic herbicides are translocated through the plant and are used to kill perennial weeds that are capable of re-growth from below-ground parts. Sometimes systemic herbicides may require more than one application to kill particularly hardy perennial weeds.

As well as herbicides that kill existing weeds, there are pre-emergence herbicides that are applied to bare soil to kill germinating weed seeds. Pre-emergence or residual herbicides may work for up to a year or more as long as the soil crust is not disturbed. These herbicides can also be used immediately after planting, on the bare ground between the ground cover plants. This can provide the ground cover plants with a chance to get established without weed competition for up to a year.

## Applying herbicides: some tips

If you decide to use herbicides, seek advice on the most suitable type for your requirements and one that will not affect the ground cover plants you are growing. Make sure you follow the safety procedures advised. Wear the appropriate clothing, as prescribed. Store all herbicides safely, especially out of reach of children and pets. Ensure you use the chemicals only at the rates advised. Spraying is best done early in the morning, before the wind gets up. Be aware that spray drift can affect other properties and damage non-target plants. Make sure you clean out spray equipment after use and safely dispose of empty containers. Ensure the safety of children, other people and pets during the spraying operation.

For small home garden operations, relatively cheap, plastic pump-action sprayers that operate on a low-volume output are ideal. Most usually hold between 5 and 10 litres of liquid. Pump up the pressure so that when the trigger is depressed a spray is produced with a moderately fine droplet. Start from the far corner of the area and work slowly back, evenly covering the weeds as you go. Do *not* spray forward and walk over what has just been sprayed. For spot-spraying weeds, wick-like applicators that can be dabbed on individual weeds may be an option. For larger areas, knapsack sprayers or larger-volume powered sprayers may be required.

## Using herbicides at different stages

As mentioned earlier, there are various different types of herbicides, which are suitable for different situations. The following is a suggested approach that could be used for weed eradication when growing ground cover plants. It includes both herbicide application and cultivation techniques.

## Before planting

To start with, use a contact or a systemic herbicide to clear the ground before cultivation. Systemic herbicides are generally best used when plants are actively growing, although for some difficult-to-control perennial weeds, such as Californian thistles (*Cirsium arvense*), systemic herbicides are most effective in the late summer to autumn period, when growth is slowing up. Others have suggested a reasonable kill can be achieved after the flowering stage. It is at this point that carbohydrates are reallocated to the perennial organs that over-winter, and it is likely that herbicides applied then will be effectively translocated to these regions of the plant. Poorer results have been observed for these difficult-to-kill plants when herbicides are used in spring. Some persistent species, such as bear's breeches (*Acanthus mollis*), even when using a systemic herbicide, will require a number of applications.

However, with these caveats in mind, a reasonable kill can be expected for most weeds from around mid-spring, with evidence of weeds beginning to die after about a week. Hot, dry summer weather and cold winter periods are not recommended for applying systemic herbicides as plants are not actively growing at these times. For contact herbicides, the effect is reasonably fast and you can expect to see evidence of annual weeds killed within two or three days at most times of the year.

After achieving early weed control by using either a contact or a systemic herbicide, cultivate the ground by turning over the soil by whatever means is available. A few weeks later, follow-up cultivation or herbicide application is important to kill any newly germinating weeds, and remove or spot spray any perennial weeds that have emerged from surviving plant material. Cultivate mechanically by rotary hoe, grubbers and harrows, or hoe and rake over the top 10 to 15 cm. Repeat over the summer as green material appears.

## Immediately post planting

Planting can be done after a final raking to remove any weed seedlings that are germinating at or near the surface. Plant out the ground cover plants at the appropriate spacing, and then tidy the area by raking the soil between the plants. At this stage there are again a number of options to make life easier in terms of weed maintenance. These include applying pre-emergence (residual) herbicides and the use of mulch. Other more intensive follow-ups to planting can be hoeing and other cultivation techniques to remove weeds, or the use of fast-colonising ground cover plants that you can expect to be overgrown at some later stage.

The use of a residual herbicide immediately or soon after planting, in conjunction with some sort of mulch applied after the herbicide, can be a very effective way of reducing after-planting care. It also ensures a reasonably weed-free environment while the target plants get established, providing them with a competitive advantage over the weeds. This method relies on having completely weed-free soil after planting and before the residual herbicide is applied.

## Post planting in established ground cover

After planting there are two likely scenarios, which will depend on whether or not a residual herbicide has been applied. If no residual herbicide is used, follow-up after planting involves removing weeds as they arrive, preferably while they are young and in the early growth stages. Weeds can be physically removed by pulling them out or hoeing the surface between the ground cover plants. Gradually, over time, as the ground cover plants grow together, the need for weeding reduces as more of the ground is shaded.

The alternative is to carefully spray between the ground cover plants to remove any weeds present. Depending on the types of weeds that are present, it may be appropriate to choose one of the selective herbicides available. Herbicide selection here will also depend to some extent on what the ground cover plants being grown are. For example, if the ground covers are all different types of native grasses and the majority of weeds are broadleaf species, it may be appropriate to choose a herbicide that selectively kills only broadleaf weeds. The reverse may apply if the weeds are mainly grass species amongst broadleaf ground cover plants.

In both of these situations, providing you have chosen a selective herbicide and have done your research, it should be safe to spray the area without being too concerned about affecting the ground cover plants. However, always exercise caution and test the herbicide chosen on a small area of ground cover plants first. If a non-selective herbicide is used, then the spraying must be done very carefully and the ground cover plants must be protected from any spray drift.

## Which herbicide should I use?

The choice of herbicides changes periodically, and some may be available only to certified approved handlers. For most people the choice of herbicides will depend on what nurseries and garden centres have available to the general public. For those who are professionally involved in the horticulture and landscape contracting areas, the range of options will be greater. Always seek advice on the best herbicides to use.

1. **Herbicides suitable for clearing weeds from ground that will be developed for planting**

   Systemic herbicides are translocated through plants and plants may take a week or more before any indications that they are dying. Perennial plants are usually killed using systemic herbicides. Contact dessicants will indicate dying plants within a day or two of application and are more effective on annual weeds.

   | Active ingredient | Trade name | Plants affected | Mode of action |
   |---|---|---|---|
   | Amitrole | Weedazol | non-selective | systemic |
   | Glyphosphate | Roundup | non-selective | systemic |
   | Glufosinate-ammonium | Buster | non-selective | contact / systemic |
   | Paraquat | Gramoxone | non-selective | contact desiccant |

2. **Pre-emergence (residual) herbicides (immediately post planting)**

   The main residual herbicides used are simazine-based and are applied to soil after planting ground cover plants. These herbicides operate by remaining close to the soil surface and killing weed seedlings as they germinate and penetrate the top few millimetres of the soil surface. Pre-emergence herbicides are applied after planting has been completed and before new weed seedlings can emerge. Do not disturb the surface of the ground after spraying because this will affect the potential of the chemical to kill weeds as they germinate. Take care to ensure ground cover plants are not affected. In particular, be aware that if used on hill sides, after heavy rainfall simazine can move from where it was applied and may wash down further into the root zone. It would be wise to exercise caution in these situations.

   | Active ingredient | Trade name | Plants affected | Mode of action |
   |---|---|---|---|
   | Simazine | Gesatop & others | non-selective | absorbed through seedling roots |

### 3. Post-planting selective herbicides to control weeds in established ground cover

There appears to be little research on the response of New Zealand native plants to specific herbicides in terms of their individual tolerance. Those interested in delving further should refer to the paper by K. C. Harrington and H. K. Schmitz on 'Initial screening of herbicides tolerated by native plants', which is listed under Useful references at the back of this book. The herbicides suggested in this paper can only be used by approved chemical applicators, but the research shows that some native species are tolerant to herbicides such as Fusilade and Gallant, which are used to kill grass weeds among some species of hebe and flax. Versatill has been shown to be effective in removing broadleaf weeds from amongst a range of species, including some New Zealand native grasses, sedges and flax.

| Active ingredient | Trade name | Plants affected | Mode of action |
| --- | --- | --- | --- |
| Fluazifop | Fusilade | grasses | systemic |
| Haloxyfop | Gallant | grasses | systemic |
| Clopyralid | Versatill | broadleaf | systemic |

# Other methods of weed control

## Using mulch after planting

Various mulches or weed mats around plants after planting can be used to maximise the period that the ground cover plants have without competition from weeds. Once they are established, the potential weed problem will diminish. Cheap and effective ways of mulching can include the use of old newspapers around plants, unless the ground cover category chosen includes spreaders, which increase by underground stems. Place about 10 or 12 sheets of newspaper around the base of the ground cover plants, as close to the stems of the plants as possible. On top of that you will need to add clean bark or something similar to hold the newspaper down. The reduced light from the mulch and newspapers will prevent weed seeds from germinating and help retain moisture around the roots of the ground cover plants. The newspaper will generally last up to a year or so before it breaks down completely. In that time the ground cover has a competitive advantage and should become well established.

## Weed removal by physical means

Where herbicide use is not an option, removal of weeds can be carried out by whatever physical means works best. In a small area a garden hoe, a garden fork or, for the odd weed in an established garden, a sturdy knife can be useful. If ground preparation and weed removal before planting are done well, subsequent weed problems are usually minimal and pulling out weeds when they are seen should not be too onerous.

Bark used as mulch around *Astelia nervosa* 'Alpine Ruby'.

# Ground cover plants

The following list of plants has been chosen by the authors as suitable for ground cover planting in a wide range of gardens throughout New Zealand. Because of the limitations on a book of this size, it does not cover the full range of possibilities, in terms of either possible species or hybrids and cultivars. The list should be seen as an introduction to the potential for greater adoption of New Zealand native plants where low-maintenance garden solutions are desired.

Left: *Fuchsia procumbens.*

## 1. *Acaena* (bidibidi, piripiri)

At the very mention of the word 'bidibidi' most people will throw up their hands in horror as they have visions of those burry seed heads that cling to woollen garments and sheep's fleeces. What many people do not realise is that there are bidibidis that have been well house-trained and would never dare to be so rash as to cling to woollen fabrics. Most of the species chosen here are well behaved.

*Acaena buchananii* is an attractive ground cover with small, sage-green leaves. Seed heads remain tucked among the leaves and do not become a pest. It is not as vigorous as some other species but has lovely foliage. (Carpet former)

*Acaena caesiiglauca* (1a) grows well in full sun, it has attractive blue-grey foliage. Seed heads are brown and are likely to catch in clothing. (Carpet former)

*Acaena dumicola* has attractive grey-green leaves edged with dark brown. Not commonly grown, it is still a fine plant. (Carpet former)

*Acaena inermis* **'Purpurea'** (1b) has attractive purple foliage and makes a very useful ground cover. It has spines on the seed heads, but without the barbs of some species that stick to your clothes. (Carpet former)

*Acaena inermis* **var.** *robusta* (1c), when in flower, has large, crimson-spined flower heads that transform its greyish mats into a glorious sight. The spines have no barbs at their tips and so it cannot become a pest. (Carpet former)

## 2. *Aciphylla* (speargrass)

### *Aciphylla dieffenbachii* (soft-leaved speargrass)

(2a) is a speargrass from the Chatham Islands. The leaves are not sharp and spiny, as one would expect from its name, but are quite soft and amenable. Indeed, its large, feathery leaves make it a handsome and graceful species. If both male and female plants are grown in proximity the female plant will reward the grower with its very ornamental, large, golden seed heads. Unfortunately, there is no way of determining the sex of individual plants until they have flowered (2b). (Sprawler)

## 3. *Anaphalioides*

*Anaphalioides* are species of everlasting flowers that have white, papery flower heads that will persist on the plants for several weeks. Some forms of *A. bellidioides* have slightly silvery leaves that really enhance the plant. They will withstand growing in the sun, but they are not desert plants and will not tolerate very dry conditions.

***Anaphalioides bellidioides*** (3a) is a prostrate and somewhat creeping species that forms trailing or creeping patches. Its small, often silvery leaves glisten in sunlight, and its white, papery, everlasting-like flower heads are a highlight during early summer. (Carpet former)

***Anaphalioides trinervis*** (3b) is a creeping or trailing plant, with leaves up to 10 cm long by 2 cm wide. The upper surface of the leaves is shiny, but not excessively so, coloured medium green, and the under surface is whitish. The flowers are white and papery, with yellow centres, and form large, long-lasting clusters. (Carpet former)

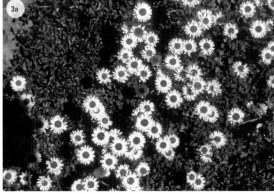

## 4.  *Anemanthele*

***Anemanthele lessoniana* (gossamer grass)** (4a) is a very attractive grass that forms bold clumps up to 80 cm or so tall by about 1 m across. It has flowing or drooping foliage, and the flowering stems are very graceful, light and feathery. (Clump former: it also spreads freely by seed but can be easily checked if necessary)

## 5.  *Arthropodium*

There are three New Zealand native species of *Arthropodium* from a genus of about 13 species in total. Other species are found in Australia, New Guinea, New Caledonia and Madagascar. *Arthropodium* species are rhizomatous perennials that may be evergreen or die down over the winter.

***Arthropodium candidum*** is a dainty little species, growing to about 30 cm tall, with small, grassy-green leaves that make it ideal for planting under trees. In shade or similar situations it is winter dormant and the new foliage appears in spring. During early summer it sends up delicate flowering stems with several small, white flowers about 10 mm across. It is a relation of the better-known *A. cirratum* or rengarenga. It prefers light shade and a moist soil, and spreads by rhizomes. (Spreader)

***Arthropodium candidum* 'Rubrum'** (5a) is a cultivar with red–purple-coloured leaves with similar characteristics to the above species. (Spreader)

***Arthropodium cirratum* (rengarenga)** (5b) is a well-known plant that grows well in semi-shade. It forms clumps of bold, large leaves that can make it quite eye-catching. It produces strong stems of attractive flowers

that are freely produced over the summer months. Nowadays there are a number of named cultivars that may be worth growing, especially those from the Three Kings Islands and the Poor Knights Islands. (Spreader)

## 6. *Asplenium*

***Asplenium bulbiferum*** (6a) is the well-known hen and chicken fern. Nowadays it is commonly confused with the hybrid and non-native *A. ✕lucrosum* (6b), which is similar, but *A. ✕lucrosum* tends to have a greater number of bulbils on each frond. *A. bulbiferum* is a robust fern that normally grows to about 60 cm to 1 m tall. It is rather variable and frequently produces bulbils (small plantlets) along its fronds, which can be removed and used for propagation. (Clump former)

***Asplenium oblongifolium*** (6c) is a strong-growing fern up to 1 m or so in height and about 1.2 m across. (Clump former)

## 7. *Astelia* (bush lily)

All astelias are generally known as bush lily, these are very handsome and adaptable plants.

***Astelia chathamica*** (7a) is a distinctive, silvery-leafed, flax-like plant that forms large clumps, up to 1.5 m tall, which are very handsome. It is a magnificent plant for the garden. One of the largest of the *Astelia* species, it has erect, broad, silvery leaves up to 2 m long by 19 cm wide, and has quite a sculptural form. If several plants are grown it is inevitable that at least one will be a female so that its orange-coloured fruits can be appreciated. Nurseries have taken to growing this species under the name 'Silver Spear', no doubt to make it more appealing to the gardener, but there is nothing to indicate that *A. chathamica* 'Silver Spear' is any different to typical forms of *A. chathamica*. (Clump former)

**Astelia fragrans** is a common but useful species of *Astelia*. It has long, green leaves up to 3 to 5 cm in width. Mature plants may be up to 1 m tall by as much across. Their leaves are curved or arch outwards and are very handsome. It is a very useful ground cover and will tolerate growing in dry situations, although it is much happier when growing in moist soils. (Clump former)

**Astelia graminea** is an attractive, small species that grows up to about 40 cm tall. It has arching, grassy leaves up to 50 cm long by up to 10 mm wide, and they are either a silvery bronze or greenish. It is an ideal smaller species that will tolerate open conditions. (Clump former)

**Astelia nervosa** (7b) is a common species that frequently occurs in hilly or mountainous regions. It is very variable, and its foliage colour varies considerably. Some forms have distinctly bronze leaves, while others may have leaves with a white, shaggy appearance, but when the scales of the furry pellicle peel they give the leaf surface a smooth appearance. (Clump former)

**Astelia nervosa 'Alpine Ruby'** (7c) is by far the best of the cultivars of *A. nervosa*, although it is still not easily obtained. It has leaves that are a lovely claret colour on their upper surfaces, while their under surfaces have a distinct sheen of silvery white. This is a truly outstanding plant. (Clump former)

**Astelia nervosa 'Nikau Red'** (7d) is similar to 'Alpine Ruby' but not quite as fine. (Clump former)

**Astelia nervosa 'Westland'** is somewhat similar to 'Alpine Ruby', but usually only some of its leaves have a purplish colour while the remainder are greenish or bronze. Some of the plants sold under this name are variable and may not be true *A. nervosa* 'Westland'. (Clump former)

**Astelia nivicola** is a distinctive and low-growing species that will grow in either sun or shade. It forms patches or colonies up to about 50 cm or more across. Its leaves are usually a silvery or greenish colour, and it can be very useful, although the highly coloured forms are more attractive to the gardener. (Clump former)

**Astelia nivicola 'Red Devil'** (7e) is similar in colour to a diminutive *A. nervosa* 'Alpine Ruby'. (Clump former)

## 8.　Blechnum

There may be up to 200 species of *Blechnum*, mainly from the southern hemisphere. They include terrestrial, epiphytic and climbing ferns. There are about 20 New Zealand species, most of which have a mixture of fertile and sterile pinnate fronds.

**Blechnum chambersii** (8a) is a handsome, medium-sized fern that has longish fronds of bright, shining green. It is a hardy fern that is easily grown in a damp, shady situation and will tolerate considerable shade. It will grow to about 40 cm tall. (Clump former)

**Blechnum discolor** (8b) grows to about 30 cm or more tall. It may often be stoloniferous, and older plants will often grow on a short trunk. Sterile fronds are up to 30 cm or more long with an upper surface bright to deep, shiny green, and a lower surface whitish to brownish. Fertile fronds are usually smaller and erect. It grows well in sun or shade. (Clump former but spreads slightly)

**Blechnum fluviatile** (8c) is quite distinct from other *Blechnum* or hard-fern species by reason of its narrow, dark-green, barren fronds growing more or less horizontally from the crown, so that they lie almost

flat on the ground. The barren fronds are about 20 cm long and spread from the crown in an almost circular fashion. Its frond segments are roundish and even in size until near the tip of the frond. The fertile fronds are quite distinct from the barren fronds (as is typical of most hard-fern species) and arise erect from the crown, growing nearly vertically to about 30 cm tall, with the segments lying almost parallel to the midrib. (Clump former)

**Blechnum montanum** is closely related to *B. novae-zelandiae*, and both are good plants to use for ground cover in the garden. *B. montanum* is a slightly smaller species, which makes it an excellent plant for slightly shady conditions, but it is hardy enough to grow even in quite open situations. Its fronds are up to 45 cm long by 25 cm wide and deep green, although the young fronds are often tinged with a red, which is always welcome during the spring months. The fertile fronds are usually held erect. (Spreader)

**Blechnum novae-zelandiae** is one of the commonest ferns of the New Zealand countryside and it may often be seen growing on road banks, on stream and river banks, and in scrublands. Under good conditions its fronds may be up to 2 m long, but under garden conditions they will usually be much shorter, up to about 40 to 60 cm. They are bright green. The sterile fronds are widest above their middles and are markedly shorter than the fertile fronds. (Spreader)

**Blechnum pennamarina** (8d) is another of the commonest of our native ferns and is easily recognised. It will quickly provide rather dense ground cover and a very attractive and handsome carpet. Its erect, fertile fronds are very distinctive, being narrower than the sterile fronds and with the segments curving downwards. The young fronds are often a reddish colour. It grows well in the shade or sun. (Spreader)

## 9. *Brachyglottis* syn. *Senecio*

This genus includes a number of evergreen, grey- or silver-green-leaved shrubs that produce bright-yellow, daisy-like flowers over summer. They are generally easy to grow in a wide range of soils and sites and can be cut back if needed. While most are best in full sun, many will tolerate shade. Although some people might baulk at the thought of using some *Brachyglottis* species for ground cover, they can be very useful provided they are treated as they should be. Some are capable of growing into large shrubs if not attended to by giving them regular pruning. *B. compacta* (9a) and *B. monroi* (9d) are two of the lower-growing kinds, whereas *B.* 'Crustii' (9b) and the *B. greyi* hybrids may grow quite a lot taller if given the chance. The problem is that many gardeners have the attitude that native plants are tough and require no maintenance. In fact they are no different to other plants and do need to be pruned in cultivation and require other regular maintenance.

**Brachyglottis compacta** (9a) has an attractive appearance. It has olive-green foliage that is slightly crimped or crenated around its flattish margins, and has a white, felted covering on its under surface. Its bright-yellow flowers form on flowering stems about 10 cm long. It usually grows to no more than 60 to 75 cm tall, although, given suitable conditions, it may grow taller. It usually requires no pruning, apart from shaping. It is fairly drought tolerant. (Hummock former)

**Brachyglottis Dunedin hybrids group** includes all hybrids between *B. compacta*, *B. laxifolia* and *B. greyi*. Most nurseries tend to regard all of these hybrids as *B. greyi*, although that species is quite rare in cultivation. Virtually everything else is of hybrid origin, in spite of what the nurseries and garden centres may call it. One of the most notable is *B.* 'Crustii' (9b), which originated in the Dunedin

Botanic Gardens. It is a shrub up to 2 m tall and as much across. It has grey-felted leaves, quite strongly crimped around their margins, and quite large clusters (about 20 to 30 cm long) of yellow flower heads. Be aware that it may or may not be correctly labelled in nurseries. *B.* 'Otari Cloud' (9c) is one of the Dunedin hybrids group that arose as a spontaneous hybrid in the Otari Plant Museum, Wellington. It has leaves covered in fine, silvery-grey hairs and has semi-double, bright-yellow flowers. It is about 1 m in height with a spread of about 1.5 m and grows best in full sun. These and all of the Dunedin hybrids group will require pruning at some time or other. The best practice is to prune off virtually all of its branches during early spring, just leaving the stumps to about 8 cm long. As spring advances, the new growth will commence to grow from the stumps that were left. (Hummock former)

*Brachyglottis monroi* (9d) is a shrub that is very similar to *B. compacta* in height and general appearance. The two can be distinguished by the crimping around the undulate leaf margins of *B. monroi*, which is much stronger than that of *B. compacta*. It usually requires only a minimum of pruning, although it may grow to 1 m tall. (Hummock former)

## 10. *Bulbinella* (Māori onion)

There are approximately 20 species, of which six are endemic to New Zealand. They are mostly winter-dormant herbaceous perennials with grass-like leaves and that have yellow flowers in late spring and early summer. Despite their common name (Māori onion), they are not at all edible.

*Bulbinella angustifolia* has narrow, green or brownish, grassy leaves and golden-yellow flower heads up to about 25 cm tall, which emerge during late spring. It is dormant in winter. (Clump former)

***Bulbinella hookeri*** (10a) is similar to *B. angustifolia* but a bolder plant, up to about 60 cm tall. It also is winter dormant. (Spreader)

## 11. Carex

*Carex* are commonly known as sedges. There are possibly up to 2000 species world-wide, and about 73 New Zealand species. Sedges are grass-like plants.

***Carex comans*** 'Frosted Curls' (11a) is a selection of *C. comans* that has very pale-green foliage that, with its bleached ends, gives the whole plant a whitish appearance. It is effective in the garden because its distinct colouring allows for some interesting planting options. (Clump former)

***Carex petriei*** is an interesting, erect species that grows to about 35 cm tall. It has a red or brownish-red colour. The true species is not always obtainable. (Clump former)

***Carex testacea*** is a handsome species because it grows to about 60 cm tall with rather arching, wide-spreading foliage that is an attractive, warm, golden-brown colour. (Clump former but may also spread by seed)

***Carex trifida*** stands out from all the others because of its bold growth and large flower heads. It will grow to a height of 80 cm or more, with wide, deep-green leaves. Its plump, brown flower spikes add to its attractiveness. (Clump former)

## 12. Celmisia (mountain daisy)

This genus comprises about 60 species of perennial herbs and sub-shrubs, most of which are New Zealand natives, with a few from South Australia and Tasmania. Celmisias are sometimes a challenge to grow. They need full sun and sharply drained soils.

***Celmisia mackaui* (Akaroa daisy)** (12a) is an attractive species of *Celmisia* that is confined to Banks Peninsula. It is a slow-growing plant but is easier to cultivate than many alpine species. It has lovely green leaves that do not have any tomentum (woolly hair) on their under surfaces, as do most other species of *Celmisia.* It will form fine clumps up to about 25 cm high, and its relatively large flowers are up to about 7 cm across. It has the added bonus that as its flowers mature they may change to a purplish-pink. (Rosette former)

***Celmisia monroi*** is an attractive, slow-growing form of the mountain daisy that is easier to maintain in cultivation than some other species. (Rosette former)

***Celmisia semicordata* var. *stricta*** (12b) is a rather desirable form of this slow-growing mountain daisy. It will form a rosette about 50 cm tall and its leaves are silvery-green. (Rosette former)

***Celmisia spectabilis*** (shepherd's daisy, puharetaiko) (12c) is a robust, tufted herb that can form clumps up to 1 m or so across. It grows best in full sun or semi-shade, with good, well-drained soils. It has leathery, lance-shaped leaves with soft, felt-like hairs on the underside. The upper surface of the leaf is deep green and shiny. Flowers are solitary, with white rays and yellow disc florets, on long stems. (Rosette former)

## 13. *Chionochloa* (snow grass)

The species of *Chionochloa* are commonly known as snow grasses and have an attractiveness that many other grasses lack. Generally they are easily grown and make a fine ground cover.

***Chionochloa conspicua* subsp. *conspicua*** forms large, flowing tussocks up to 1 m tall when flowering and makes a fine feature, especially when it produces its lovely flowering plumes, which may be up to 1.8 m tall. (Clump former)

***Chionochloa flavicans*** (13a) resembles a slightly smaller version of the former. It will grow to about 1 m tall with flowing green foliage and produces large, conspicuous flower plumes, which makes it resemble a miniature toetoe. Its flowering plumes remain attractive for several months. (Clump former)

***Chionochloa rubra*** (**red tussock**) (13b) is a very commonly cultivated species of *Chionochloa*. It is handsome and hardy, and will cope with windy situations. It will grow to a metre or more in height and forms lovely flowing tussocks of a greenish-tawny to reddish-tawny colour. (Clump former)

## 14. Coprosma

There is a moderate range of coprosmas that are suitable for ground cover planting. All are evergreen species and grow best in full sun. Coprosmas normally fit into either carpet formers, sprawlers or hummock formers. Some start as carpet formers and end up growing into bun-shaped plants as the long, trailing shoots grow over older shoots.

***Coprosma acerosa*** **'Hawera'** (14a) forms a bright-green-leaved, usually prostrate, dense bush. (Carpet former)

***Coprosma atropurpurea*** forms a wide-spreading, rather dense mat up to a metre or more across. The tips of its leaves are dark, which makes it more conspicuous when grown against suitable contrasting plants. Both male and female plants are required if it is to produce its attractive, port-wine-coloured fruits. (Carpet former, sometimes with age appearing more like a hummock former)

***Coprosma brunnea*** (14b) is a relatively fast-growing, trailing, much-branched shrub that does well in full sun. It has a yellowish-bronze appearance and either blue or translucent, blue-speckled fruits during summer. (Carpet former)

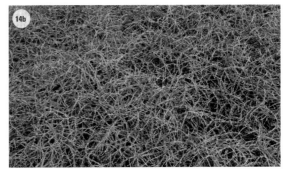

*Coprosma* ✕*kirkii* 'Kirkii' (14c) is a vigorous, rapidly growing bush that does best in full sun but will tolerate light shade. It is a much-branched, more or less prostrate ground cover but eventually may mound up to become more of a hummock as the long branches tend to grow over others below. This plant stands pruning very well. (Carpet former, sprawler or sometimes with age appearing more like a hummock former)

*Coprosma petriei* is very similar to *C. atropurpurea* but it has pale-blue fruits. (Carpet former, sometimes with age appearing more like a hummock former)

*Coprosma propinqua* var. *martinii* 'Taiko' (14d) was named after the rare Chatham Islands petrel by Graeme Platt. This is a quick-growing carpeting ground cover similar in habit to *C.* ✕*kirkii*. (Carpet former, sometimes with age appearing more like a hummock former)

*Coprosma* 'Wharariki Beach' (14e) is a cultivar from Wharariki Beach near Cape Farewell selected by Mike Crawford. This appears to have *C. repens* as one parent, but we are uncertain of what else makes up this hybrid form. This is a carpeting ground cover with dense foliage and it grows quickly. (Carpet former, sometimes with age appearing more like a hummock former)

## 15. Dianella

These are useful plants that look like smaller kinds of New Zealand flaxes (*Phormium*). Although they do not have attractive flowers, their small flowers are followed by attractive berries.

*Dianella haematica* is somewhat larger than *D. nigra*. It produces clumps of foliage up to about 50 cm tall that resemble miniature flax. It has branched flowering stems up to 75 cm long, on which very attractive blue fruits form. It is quite hardy and will even tolerate a certain amount of drought. (Clump former)

*Dianella nigra* (15a) resembles a miniature flax. It is a tufted plant growing to about 30 to 40 cm tall. Its flowering stems are shorter than those of *D. haematica* and its fruits vary in colour from almost white to a lovely blue. If propagated by division, the fruit colour may be selected so that only good forms are secured for growing. (Clump former)

*Dianella nigra* **'Margaret Pringle'** (15b) has leaves that are longitudinally variegated with creamy stripes. (Clump former)

## 16. Disphyma

There are thought to be four species in this genus of evergreen, trailing succulent plants, two of which are endemic to New Zealand.

*Disphyma australe* **(horokaka)** (16a) is commonly found throughout New Zealand in coastal areas, and makes an excellent ground cover plant in drier situations, providing that frosts are not too severe. (Carpet former)

## 17. Doodia

*Doodia australis* **(pukupuku)** (17a) is one of the commonest of our native fern species in the North Island. It has rather firm fronds that grow up to 60 cm long, are rather harsh to the touch, and with up to 50 pairs of leaflets. The fronds are a lovely pink or reddish colour, particularly when young, eventually maturing to green. It sends out stolons so that it will soon fill a larger area. It will grow in open situations or light shade. (Spreader)

## 18. Elatostema

*Elatostema rugosum* **(parataniwha)** (18a) is an attractive herbaceous plant for growing in shady situations in a moist soil. It will grow up to a metre or so tall, but often a bit less. Its stems have leaves alternating along each side, and they are up to 25 cm long and usually a brownish- or bronzy-green. Its flowers are minute, forming hemispherical little balls up to 2 cm in diameter. It is frost tender but can be

grown in frostier climates if given sufficient protection. (Spreader)

## 19. Euphorbia

**Euphorbia glauca (shore spurge, waiū-atua)** (19a, with golden pīngao in the background) is now becoming rarer because of habitat destruction. *E. glauca* is an attractive herbaceous plant for growing in open situations. It sends up erect stems, up to a metre tall, furnished with grey or glaucous leaves up to 10 cm long by 2.5 cm wide. Its flowers are produced from the tips of its stems and are an attractive reddish colour. (Spreader)

## 20. Fuchsia

**Fuchsia procumbens (creeping fuchsia)** (20a) grows prostrate along the ground and is excellent where a trailing plant is required. It has thin, branched, wiry stems with bright-green leaves about the size of a large fingernail. In summer the flowers are a feature of this plant. Plants have either male or female flowers. The male flowers are attractively coloured (yellow and purple changing to greenish as they age) and produce bright-blue pollen. The female flowers are similar in colour to the male but lack the bright-blue pollen. Another feature of the female plants is the large, red berries that sit above the foliage. (Spreader)

## 21. Gaultheria (snowberry)

**Gaultheria depressa var. depressa** (21a) is an attractive little shrub that grows to about 10 cm tall. It has small, roundish leaves. Because its flower buds are formed during the previous summer, it can flower quite early the following spring. Its fruits may be white, pink or red, and so if particular coloured fruits are required it should be vegetatively propagated. The 'fruits' of the snowberry are not fruits in the accepted sense but are actually the swollen calyces of the flower, which swell around the ovules so that it resembles a succulent berry. (Carpet former)

***Gaultheria depressa*** var. ***novae-zelandiae*** is similar to the former but differs in having a more matted habit and can be a little taller. It grows up to about 12 cm tall. It is found along the eastern side of the South Island, and frequently has only white fruits. (Carpet former)

## 22. Geranium

The native geraniums are handsome herbaceous plants that are useful for ground cover effects. Most will grow in open situations, and a couple have attractive flowers.

***Geranium microphyllum* 'Discolor'** is a very distinctive form of one of the native geraniums. It is a small, creeping plant that has small, rounded leaves that are bronze-green and mottled with yellow-green, making it easily distinguishable. During summer it produces small, white flowers. (Carpet former)

***Geranium sessiliflorum*** is closely allied to *G. microphyllum* but is not creeping because it arises from a single tap root. It will form clumps up to about 15 cm tall by perhaps 25 cm across. There are two forms of this species: one with green leaves and the other with attractive bronze leaves ('Purpureum', 22a). Both forms seed freely, although any unwanted seedlings are quite easily removed. (Rosette former)

***Geranium traversii*** comes from the Chatham Islands and is the finest of our native geranium species. It will form a plant up to 12 cm or so in height and may grow to about 40 cm across. It has light-green or grey-green leaves up to about 7.5 cm in diameter, and over the summer it produces liberal quantities of pink flowers about 2.5 cm across. (Carpet former)

***Geranium* 'Pink Spice'** (22b) is a selected cultivar from a hybrid cross between *G. traversii* (and probably *G. sessiliflorum*). This cultivar has bronzy foliage and attractive pink flowers. (Carpet former)

## 23. Geum

**Geum cockaynei,** formerly known as *G. parviflorum*, is an attractive plant for growing in quantity in a moist and shady situation. It will grow to about 10 cm tall, or up to about 30 cm when in flower. Its leaves are usually wide spreading and have one large terminal leaflet. Its white flowers are up to 1.5 cm in diameter and there are several on the stem. (Clump former)

## 24. Gingidia

**Gingidia montana** is a distinctive and easily recognised species. It has bold foliage, with up to 10 pairs of broad leaflets that are a bright, shiny green. In flower it will grow to about 50 cm tall, and its heads of small, white flowers are very attractive. It has one disadvantage in that aphids (sucking insects) are often attracted to it. (Clump former)

## 25. Gunnera

The following native species of *Gunnera* grow flat on the ground and usually form a tight ground cover. Some of the species have very attractive fruits.

**Gunnera hamiltonii** (25a) is one of the best of several species of *Gunnera* that are suitable for the garden. It is a rare species, from Southland and Stewart Island. One of the largest of our native gunneras, it has attractive, bronzy leaves that are shovel-shaped. It creeps along the ground and the leaves are produced from each node. When growing well it makes a fine ground cover. (Carpet former)

**Gunnera monoica** is one of the commonest of the native species of *Gunnera*. It grows in many parts of the country and will form a very good ground cover when grown in a damp or shady situation. *G. monoica*

has small, rounded, green leaves with toothed margins. It will produce white fruits, but they will seldom be a noticeable feature of the plant. (Carpet former)

***Gunnera prorepens*** is a distinct and easily recognised species that will form good mats of foliage. Its leaves are larger than those of *G. monoica* and are often brownish or purplish. The leaf blade may be up to 6 cm long by 4 cm wide. It will produce 6 cm long spikes of red to purplish fruits that are quite attractive during the late summer. (Carpet former)

## 26. Haloragis

***Haloragis erecta*** **(toatoa)** is a soft-wooded perennial or sub-shrub that is fast growing and soon provides a dense ground cover about 50 cm high. Its flowers are small and not particularly significant. This species seems to grow well in either full sun or moderately shady sites. The Māori name, toatoa, is also used for species of *Phyllocladus*. (Hummock former)

***Haloragis erecta*** **'Wanganui Bronze'** (incorrectly known as 'Wellington Bronze') (26a) is a cultivar with dark, bronze-purple leaves and stems. (Hummock former)

## 27. Hebe

This is a large and well-recognised group of plants whose nomenclature has been somewhat unstable. It was originally classified as *Veronica*, then changed to *Hebe*, then more latterly separated into several genera, retaining some as *Hebe* but separating others from *Hebe* into *Heliohebe*, *Leonohebe* and *Parahebe*, all belonging to the family Scrophulariaceae. Recent further changes suggest that all now belong in the family Plantaginaceae and should revert to their former generic name of *Veronica*. Within this group of plants we have been very selective, recognising that there are many others that could have been

chosen. Most have interesting leaf colour as well as attractive flowering characteristics. They are easy to grow, do best in full sun or light shade only, and tolerate pruning or cutting back if needed. Most are soft-wooded shrubs or sub-shrubs, often fast growing, and are relatively free of pests and diseases. In general, the larger-leaved forms do better in coastal, lowland areas of New Zealand, as they tend to be sensitive to frost, while the smaller-leaved forms tend to be hardier. The latter include the whipcord forms, which resemble dwarf conifers in many respects, until they produce flowers! The smaller-leaved hebes are generally more tolerant of colder, drier conditions.

***Hebe armstrongii*** (27a) is a bun-shaped shrub with an overall bronze or yellow-green appearance. It is a whipcord hebe that is commonly grown in gardens and is easily obtained. It has white flowers in summer but does not always flower well in cultivation and is mainly grown for its unusual foliage colour and

textural qualities. This is a hardy species, well suited to cooler, drier climates. (Hummock former)

***Hebe buchananii*** (27b) is a slow-growing, grey-leaved hebe suitable for smaller gardens. It has white flowers in late spring or early summer. In time it may grow to about 30 cm high, with a spread of two or three times that. (Hummock former)

***Hebe chathamica*** (27c) trails across the ground with a somewhat loose habit of growth. It provides a dense ground cover of up to 30 to 40 cm high with a spread of many times that. It is a useful plant where trailing over a wall or bank is required. Flowers are white to violet and usually occur from early to mid-summer. (Carpet former)

***Hebe decumbens*** (27d) is a good ground cover for smaller gardens, growing to about 25 cm or so high with a reasonable rate of growth. It can easily be cut back if it outgrows its allotted area. *H. decumbens* flowers around late spring or early summer. The flowers are pure white and contrast strongly with the

dark-green, red-margined leaves and black stems of this species. (Carpet former)

***Hebe* ✕*franciscana* 'Lobelioides'** (syn. 'Blue Gem') (27e) is a larger-growing hebe that can provide a good, dense ground cover between 1 and 2 m high. It is an excellent coastal plant and also seems to be quite hardy in some inland areas, such as parts of Canterbury. This cultivar can be used in larger gardens. It flowers for long periods: the bulk of flowering occurs over the summer, but often continues through the autumn and at other periods during the year. Flowers are usually a strong violet-blue colour. (Hummock former)

***Hebe* ✕*franciscana* 'Silver Queen'** (incorrectly known as 'Waireka') (27f) is a cultivar with variegated leaves. It is not as vigorous as 'Lobelioides', and reaches little more than a third of the height and spread of 'Lobelioides'. (Hummock former)

***Hebe obtusata*** (27g) is a similar species in terms of its habit of growth to *H. chathamica*, but the leaves and flowers tend to be larger. Flowers are presented in long, lateral racemes and coloured mauve to white. This plant is more or less prostrate, but tends to sprawl across the ground. It is useful where a plant that trails down over a wall or bank is needed. (Carpet former)

***Hebe odora* (boxwood)** (27h) is a commonly grown, bun-shaped species that in gardens tends to form a rounded shrub of about 1 m in height and spread. White flowers are produced in late spring or early summer. It is a hardy species that needs little in the way of attention. (Hummock former)

***Hebe pinguifolia*** (27i) is an under-utilised plant. This is a variable species that grows in drier areas. There are two cultivars, 'Pagei' and 'Sutherlandii', which are low-growing, silver-leaved forms and are ideal carpeting ground covers. Each of the cultivars will grow up to a metre or so in diameter with a height of only about 20 cm. Eventually their height will vary to produce a sculpted effect, which can be visually interesting. (Carpet former)

***Hebe topiara*** (27j) is a good species for mass planting where a height of about 75 cm or less is required. This ball-shaped shrub has small, blue-grey leaves, and as a single specimen retains its shape well and has a clipped appearance, hence the specific epithet alluding to topiary – the garden act of clipping trees or shrubs into formal or other shapes. (Hummock former)

## 28. Heliohebe

***Heliohebe hulkeana* (New Zealand lilac)** (28a) is an attractive plant that grows into a bushy shrub up to about 70 cm tall. It can be much branched and should be given sufficient space to spread so that it is not over-crowded. It flowers in mid-spring, producing attractive sprays of pale mauve flowers that terminate the stems. (Hummock former)

***Heliohebe hulkeana* 'Lena'** is an attractive, compact, white-flowered cultivar of *H. hulkeana.* (Hummock former)

***Heliohebe* 'Hagley Park'** (28b) is a very attractive, smaller plant with pink flowers. It is a cultivar from a cross between *H. hulkeana* and *H. raoulii.* (Hummock former)

## 29. Jovellana

***Jovellana sinclairii*** (29a) is a sub-shrub species that grows to about 45 cm high, with largish oval leaves that are soft green and make a pleasant foil for its flowers. The flowers are produced in branched panicles up to 45 cm long. Individual flowers are similar to those of a small-flowered calceolaria. The white flowers have purple spots inside and are flushed with yellow in the throat. (Sprawler)

## 30. Lastreopsis

This is a genus of up to 35 species of mainly terrestrial ferns, characterised by their often-distinct, five-angled fronds. There are four species native to New Zealand with triangular-shaped fronds.

**Lastreopsis glabella** is a very attractive native fern that is an excellent garden plant. It is a tufted species with triangular fronds that are deep green, with reddish-brown hairs on the upper surfaces. It grows to about 45 cm high and is a very neat plant. (Spreader)

**Lastreopsis velutina** (30a) is a somewhat larger species than *L. glabella* and has a broadly triangular frond that is also a deep green but is covered with fine, brownish hairs that give the whole frond a velvety appearance. It will grow to about 60 cm high, or even more. (Spreader)

## 31. Leptinella

There are approximately 33 species of *Leptinella*, most of which are endemic to New Zealand. These are a good choice for smaller gardens.

**Leptinella calcarea** will make a fine, compact, carpeting plant that will end up a metre or more across. It spreads by underground rhizomes and has finely cut leaves that are medium green. It will soon form a light-green carpet and will grow in almost any well-drained soil. It also withstands quite dry conditions. (Spreader)

**Leptinella pyrethrifolia** is not nearly as vigorous as *L. calcarea* but it will form attractive mats of light- to medium-green foliage that have an attractive scent. Its leaves tend to be scattered along the stem but are mainly clustered towards the tips. Its flowers stand up above the foliage on 10 cm stalks, each of which bears a rounded, button-shaped flower head of creamy yellow. (Spreader)

**Leptinella squalida** is a common but nevertheless attractive species. The normal form has bright-green, or sometimes brownish, feathery leaves and it will soon form a dense carpet that only some of the more persistent weeds are able to gain a foothold in. It has small flower heads up to 5 mm in diameter. It will soon spread to cover several metres of ground. (Spreader)

**Leptinella squalida 'Platt's Black'** (31a) is a form discovered by Graham Platt of Auckland. Its leaves are an almost overall blackish colour. (Spreader)

## 32. Leptospermum

**Leptospermum scoparium (mānuka)** is a widespread shrub found throughout much of New Zealand. They are attractive in flower. Most mānuka are likely to be affected by scale insects and may need to be sprayed occasionally to deal with this pest. Mānuka can also be pruned if required. There are some cultivars that can be used for ground cover. Two options are the carpeting or sprawling 'Red Falls' (32a,b), which has dark-red flowers in spring, and the pink-flowered, bun-shaped 'Huia' (32c). However, there are many other cultivars that could be considered.

## 33. Libertia

There are about 20 species of *Libertia*, which are mainly rhizomatous perennial herbs. The five or so New Zealand species are all endemic. All have white flowers, ornamental seed capsules and leathery leaves.

**Libertia grandiflora** is similar to *L. ixioides* but it lacks the foliage colour of that species. It will form a clump up to 50 cm or so in height and it has narrow, green leaves, but when it flowers the flower stems stand well above the foliage so that it makes a splendid display. When ripe, its seed capsules usually turn blackish. (Clump former)

**Libertia ixioides (New Zealand iris, mīkoikoi)** is the common so-called 'native' iris. It is a densely tufted plant with a stiff habit of growth, growing to about 50 cm tall. It has medium-green leaves with a thickened midrib up the centre. During spring or early summer it sends up branched flowering stems that bear several white, iris-like flowers, each about 2 cm across (33a). After flowering it produces its ornamental seed capsules that turn an attractive orange as they ripen (33b). Some forms have much larger seed capsules than others. It is worth trying to obtain one of the larger-fruited forms. (Clump former)

*Libertia ixioides* **'Taupo Blaze'** is an attractive cultivar that was bred at the Taupo Native Plant Nursery. Its leaves are a warm, brownish colour, while its wide midribs are orange. The whole effect is very pleasing. (Clump former)

*Libertia ixioides* **'Taupo Sunset'** is similar to 'Taupo Blaze' but the overall leaf colour is a little more greyish. (Clump former)

*Libertia peregrinans* (33c) makes an excellent ground cover, except that it has the bad habit of trying to escape from wherever it has been planted and trying to grow somewhere else. It is rather like the kitchen-garden mint in that it needs to be confined to an escape-proof container. If it can be accommodated in a suitable part of the garden, where it can be kept in check, it can be a very effective plant. Its foliage tends to be orange for most of the year and it is not the most prolific flowerer, but that is more than compensated for by its fine display of foliage. (Spreader)

## 34. Lobelia

These plants are now classified within *Lobelia* but formerly were known to gardeners as *Pratia*. Alas, they will now have to think of them as *Lobelia*.

*Lobelia angulata* **(pānakenake)** grows fairly rapidly and will soon creep out to form a reasonably dense mat of foliage. Over the summer months it produces numerous white flowers (34a) that do actually resemble those of the familiar garden lobelia. During late summer or autumn they produce attractive, purplish-red fruits (34b) that last for a long time on the plant. (Carpet former)

*Lobelia macrodon*, while not nearly such a rapid grower as *L. angulata,* is a delightful plant. It has shiny leaves, and its pale creamy or yellowish flowers have a delightful perfume that scents the surrounding air and can be detected on any warm day when one is close enough. (Carpet former)

## 35. Machaerina

***Machaerina sinclairii*** (35a) grows into large, leafy clumps with shiny, iris-like foliage. On well-grown plants its leaves may be up to 1.5 m long by 3 cm wide. Its rigid flowering stems are up to a metre long and are much branched, with attractive red-brown or rusty-brown spikelets. This is an ideal plant for shade, or moist sites. (Clump former)

## 36. Mazus

***Mazus novae-zeelandiae*** **subsp.** *impolitus* **'Matapouri Bay'** (36a) is a cultivar from Matapouri Bay in Northland that has pale-blue flowers on erect stems above the foliage in summer. It grows best in slight shade in moist soils. (Spreader)

***Mazus radicans*** is an easily recognised species that forms dense mats. The leaves have dark markings or mottling on their upper surfaces. During early summer it produces liberal quantities of attractive flowers,

which resemble a cloud of butterflies that have come to rest on the foliage. The flowers have a small upper lip flushed with purple and a larger, white lower lip with yellow inside its throat. Later in the season its purplish-red fruiting capsules begin to ripen and they remain on the plant for some time. (Carpet former)

## 37. Metrosideros

There are about 20 evergreen species in this genus, including the mainly red-flowering pōhutakawa and rātā trees. The genus also includes climbing plants and some shrubs. Most are not suitable for ground cover and are sensitive to frosts, but the following cultivar of the normally climbing species *M. carminea* could be considered.

***Metrosideros carminea*** **'Ferris Wheel'** (37a) is a compact-growing shrub propagated from the adult form of *M. carminea* that has an attractive flowering display. (Hummock former)

### 38. Microlaena

*Microlaena avenacea* **(bush rice-grass)** (38a) is a very pleasing grass that is well worth a place in almost any garden. It has drooping to somewhat spreading foliage and grows to about 60 cm tall. Its drooping flower panicles are pale to deepish-green, and its flower stems are quite dainty. It occurs naturally in the North, South, Stewart and Auckland Islands. (Clump former)

### 39. Microsorum

*Microsorum pustulatum* **(hound's tongue, kōwaowao)** (39a) is a rather common and very hardy fern that is useful as a ground cover. Formerly classified as *Phymatosorus diversifolius*, it has now been determined that it should be known as *Microsorum pustulatum*. It is a creeping fern with very tough foliage and prominent clusters of orange spores on the backs of its fronds. The spore masses cause the upper surface to appear as though the frond has numerous pustules on its upper surface. The bright-green, shiny fronds are variously shaped and lobed, and it will happily grow in the ground under the shade of trees and shrubs and will provide an excellent ground cover. (Spreader)

### 40. Myosotidium

*Myosotidium hortensia* **(Chatham Island forget-me-not)** (40a) is easily recognised by its large leaves that are marked by strong ribs radiating out from the leaf stalk. It grows to about 60 cm or more in height and will form clumps about 1 m across. As a foliage plant alone it is quite spectacular, but when it flowers during early spring it can be truly magnificent, with large, prominent flower heads. The commonest form, and the one usually grown, has bright-blue flowers that become a deeper blue towards their centres. In another form the flowers are broadly margined with white around the flower lobes. (Clump former)

## 41. *Myosotis* (forget-me-not)

There are about 50 species in this genus of annual, biennial, creeping or tufted perennial herbs world-wide. About 34 species are endemic to New Zealand, some of which have showy flowers.

***Myosotis eximia*** (41a) is one of the finest species of our native forget-me-nots and is a great species to use as a ground cover. It will form large patches up to 50 cm across and is easily grown in a semi-shady situation (not with directly overhead shade though). Its leaves are a bluish green and it has large, white flowers that contrast attractively against the foliage. Normally it will flower from October until February. It occurs naturally in the Ruahine and Kaimanawa Ranges in the North Island. (Clump former)

***Myosotis petiolata*** has several varieties, but the one that appears to be the most commonly available is *M. petiolata* var. *pottsiana*, which comes from the Opotiki area. Its rosette leaves are up to about 2.5 cm in diameter and its flowers up to about 12 mm in diameter. Its leaves are a fresh green and tend to form

open clumps. An ideal plant for growing in wooded situations, it will also tolerate being grown in the open. In the garden it will grow to about 12 cm tall and its stems normally carry a number of white flowers. It may also produce some flowers through the autumn or winter months. Although this species tends to seed itself around the garden, it is an easily tolerated plant that is usually welcome rather than being a nuisance. (Clump former)

## 42. *Myrsine*

***Myrsine nummularia*** (42a) is a small, low-growing shrub that under good conditions may spread to cover a metre or more. It has small, rounded leaves about 10 mm across. Usually they are a pale to deep reddish-brown, and their colour is considerably accentuated during the colder months of the year. It has minute flowers, and the male and female flowers are on separate plants. If one grows both male and female plants the female bush will reward the grower with its very attractive, violet-coloured fruits. It will grow in full sun or semi-shade. (Carpet former)

### 43. Nertera

**Nertera depressa** is the commonest species of *Nertera*, and when in fruit it is very attractive. It is a small, creeping herb with tiny, shiny-green leaves. Its flowers are minute, but when they are replaced by the attractive bright-red fruits it is something to behold. *N. depressa* is not vigorous enough to withstand competition from other plants or weeds, but it is worth giving it some care and attention in order to maintain it. (Carpet former)

### 44. Pachystegia

This is a genus of three endemic New Zealand species. All are woody shrubs that have attractive, large, leathery leaves and attractive, large, daisy-like flowers in summer.

**Pachystegia insignis (Marlborough rock daisy)** (44a) is a sun-loving plant that grows in the east coast of the South Island from the Awatere to North Canterbury. It has large, attractive leaves and tends to grow into a flattish bun-shaped shrub of up to a metre in spread and a little less in height. It has drumstick-like flower heads in mid-summer. (Hummock former)

### 45. Parahebe

There are approximately 30 species of *Parahebe* world-wide. They are typically evergreen, prostrate sub-shrubs and have attractive, showy flowers.

**Parahebe decora** is one of the more common species of parahebe and may be found along just about every mountain stream. It is usually a prostrate shrub, but not densely growing, and may be recognised by its dark stems and minute, often-reddish leaves, with usually a pair of notches on either side of their margins. The flowering stems stand well above the rest of the plant so that they almost appear to be out of proportion to the size of the plant. Each inflorescence has about 10 to 15 bowl-shaped flowers that vary from white to pink, with violet and darker lines. (Carpet former)

**Parahebe hookeriana 'Olsenii'** is a small, prostrate species that occurs on the Ruahine Range of the North Island. It has rather compact growth and may not be as wide spreading as *P. decora*, but it is a very worthwhile species. Its flowers are a fine shade of pink, and it flowers for a long time. (Carpet former)

**Parahebe lyallii** (45a) has a variable habit, but it is usually prostrate and most varieties are creeping and rooting. Its small leaves have about three notches around their margins. Its inflorescences are not as stiff and erect as those of *P. decora*. Flower colour may vary from white to pink, with darker lines inside the flower. (Carpet former)

## 46. Phormium

There are two species of flax (*P. colensoi* and *P. tenax*) and numerous hybrids and cultivars of varying heights and spreads. Many have variegated or single colours, from greens through to pinks, yellows to deep purple, reds or bronze, for example *Phormium* 'Pink Panther' (46a) and *Phormium* 'Sunset' (46b). There are some variegated cultivars that are unstable and likely to revert. If you see distinctly different leaf colours in the clump you are buying, it may pay to ask if they are stable. Flaxes are clump formers and some care should be taken not to plant these too close to paths, as the leaves of the lax mountain flax in particular can become a tripping hazard. The two species hybridise freely.

**Phormium colensoi** syn. **P. cookianum** (mountain flax, wharariki) (46c) is recognised by generally having leaves that tend to droop from halfway, green and yellow flowers, and seed pods that point toward the ground and are spirally twisted on the flower stem (46d). (Clump former)

***Phormium tenax* (New Zealand flax, harakeke)** (46e) is recognised by generally having leaves and seed pods that are erect. Flowers tend to be red. (Clump former)

## 47. Pimelea

*Pimelea* are reminiscent of *Hebe* – until they flower. They are attractive shrubs that can be very useful as ground covers. The various species of *Pimelea* provide some extremely useful and effective garden plants. Generally, they are more tolerant of adverse conditions than are many of the hebes.

***Pimelea aridula*** (47a) is an excellent ground cover plant because it will tolerate very dry conditions and, at times, also quite wet conditions. It forms a bush up to 40 cm high and may eventually grow up to 1.5 m across. It forms very dense growth and will make an attractive ground cover. It has the added advantage that it is almost never without a flower, even if only just a few. It has small, greyish-green leaves and its white flowers are in compact heads at the tips of its branchlets. (Carpet former)

***Pimelea mimosa*** (47b) was previously known by the cultivar name of 'Silver Ghost', but has now been correctly named as *P. mimosa*. It grows naturally on Te Mata Peak in Hawke's Bay. It has attractive, silvery foliage and has quite a long flowering period. It forms a bush up to 40 cm high by about 1.5 m across and has the added advantage of seldom being without some flowers, even when the flowering season may appear to be over. It is easily cultivated in a dryish situation and will tolerate occasional periods of wet conditions. (Carpet former)

***Pimelea prostrata*** (pinātoro) is a small, prostrate, mat-forming species that has dark-brown branches and small leaves of blue-green or grey-green. Its flower heads are produced from the tips of the branchlets. It is a fairly tough plant that will withstand considerable dryness and is common around coastal areas. (Carpet former)

*Pimelea prostrata* **'Blue Peter'** (47c) is a form collected from around the Auckland area. It has slightly larger leaves, which are a distinct bluish-grey colour, and it is a good plant for the garden. (Carpet former)

*Pimelea* **'Quicksilver'** (47d) is an attractive cultivar of unknown parentage that was collected from the Mercury Islands by well-known nurseryman Terry Hatch. It is an attractive, bushy plant that usually grows to about 20 cm in height and has grey-green or slightly glaucous foliage with a rather silvery appearance. Its white flower heads are usually produced in profusion, and there is hardly a time of the year when it has no flowers on show. (Carpet former)

*Pimelea traversii* (47e) is a small, rounded shrub that grows to about 70 cm in height and spread. It has

masses of white flower heads in summer and attractive grey-green leaves. (Carpet former)

*Pimelea urvilleana* is similar to *P. prostrata* and is an excellent ground cover. It forms a dense carpet. (Carpet former)

## 48. Pittosporum

*Pittosporum tenuifolium* **(kōhūhū)** is a species that embraces a diversity of forms, and while the taller, tree-like forms may be too large to consider as ground cover, there are newer cultivars that form ball-like shrubs and may attain heights of only up to 1 m. Cultivars that could be useful include 'Golf Ball' (48a) (of hybrid origin), an attractive, shiny-leaved round form, and 'Tom Thumb' (48b), a less-formal and broader-shaped cultivar with dark-purple leaves. (Hummock former)

## 49. Polystichum

*Polystichum* is a genus of about 175 species of terrestrial ferns world-wide that have erect, scaly fronds. There are about seven species endemic to New Zealand.

**Polystichum richardii (common shield fern)** (49a) is a very hardy fern that will tolerate fairly adverse conditions. It has bi- or tripinnate, compound fronds and the base of the midribs are covered in blackish-brown scales. It occurs in forests and scrublands throughout New Zealand. (Clump former)

**Polystichum vestitum (prickly shield fern)** (49b) is a hardy and very handsome fern for ground cover purposes. It has firm, deep-green fronds up to 1 m long by 25 cm wide, with chaffy-brown scales along the midrib (49c). It is excellent for shady situations and is not too fussy about soil. (Clump former)

## 50. Raoulia

This genus comprises 20 or so endemic New Zealand evergreen shrubs or perennial herbs. They all require fall sun and good drainage. The shrubby species of *Raoulia* include the well-known 'vegetable sheep', which forms quite large, dense mats.

**Raoulia australis (golden mat daisy)** is a silvery colour, and when it flowers the whole mat becomes bright yellow. The tips of its growth are quite densely placed so that it is not possible for weeds to gain much of a footing. *R. australis* is only suitable for open situations. (Carpet former)

**Raoulia hookeri (patch plant)** (50a) is a variable species, with some forms being more attractive for the garden than others. It also forms a mat of silvery foliage but its flower heads are creamy instead of yellow. Some forms of this species have a rather loose

habit of growth and are not as attractive as garden plants as are others. One very good form is *R. hookeri* 'Makara', so-named because it was collected from Makara Beach near Wellington. It has larger leaves that are more silvery, which gives it a bolder appearance than other forms of this species. (Carpet former)

***Raoulia tenuicaulis* (tutahuna)** is one of the commonest species of *Raoulia* and it will cover extensive areas of ground. It forms silvery-green mats and has cream to whitish flower heads. If allowed to grow unchecked it may cover an area of up to 2 or 3 square metres. (Carpet former)

## 51. Rubus

There are thought to be around 250 species in this genus world-wide and about six species endemic to New Zealand. Most species are typically thorny, and scrambling or climbing perennials. The New Zealand species are commonly called bush lawyer.

***Rubus X barkeri*** (51a) is a useful ground cover with bronze-green leaves that grows well in a variety of situations. Because each plant will eventually cover a large area, it is not recommended for smaller gardens. It does not flower or fruit as it is a hybrid between the more aggressive *R. australis* and *R. parvus*. (Carpet former)

## 52. Samolus

***Samolus repens* (māakoako)** (52a) is a dainty species that is mainly a coastal plant. It may be recognised by its prostrate or sprawling habit and by its slightly fleshy leaves and white flowers. Its leaf blades are up to 15 mm long by 8 mm wide, and its white flowers are up to 12 mm in diameter. It will grow in almost any soil, although it prefers it to be reasonably moist. (Carpet former)

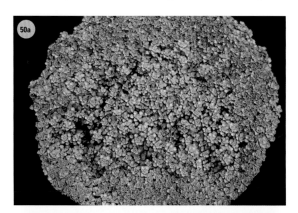

## 53. Scleranthus

*Scleranthus* species form very attractive cushions that resemble a moss, but they are in fact in the same family as the carnation.

**Scleranthus biflorus (kohukohu)** (53a) is by far the most commonly grown species and it will, in suitable conditions, grow into a spreading cushion up to 2 m or so across. It forms lovely, green, hummocky, 'mossy' cushions that will deter most invasive plants from gaining foothold or roothold. (Carpet former)

**Scleranthus uniflorus**, apart from its ultimate size and its colour, is almost identical to *S. biflorus.* It is usually a yellowish-green and seldom attains the dimensions of *S. biflorus,* being a much smaller plant. (Carpet former)

## 54. Scutellaria

**Scutellaria novae-zelandiae** (54a) is a small, semi-woody species, growing up to about 30 cm tall, which normally inhabits wooded alluvial areas, particularly adjacent to streams and rivers. It has small, deep-green leaves and its white flowers may be produced over a long period. (Sprawler)

## 55. Selliera

**Selliera radicans** (remuremu) (55a) is a coastal species, making it a good ground cover plant. It is a mat-forming plant that has spoon-shaped or club-shaped leaves, and its white flowers are split along one side, giving them a curiously one-sided appearance. Its flowers are scented and are normally produced over a period of two to three months. Under good conditions it will cover an area of several square metres. (Carpet former)

## 56. *Sophora* (kōwhai)

Kōwhai is regarded by many to be New Zealand's national flower. Kōwhai are an easily recognised group of plants, but accurate species identification can be difficult because many species hybridise freely with one another. Kōwhai have alternately arranged, pinnately compound leaves and showy flowers in varying shades of yellow. There are currently thought to be eight New Zealand species and possibly a further 40–50 species from places as diverse as Chile, Mexico, China, the Himalayas and Hawaii. Two New Zealand species are included here as being suitable for ground cover plants because of their smaller size and shrubby nature.

***Sophora molloyi*** is an evergreen shrub that tends to spread more in width than it grows in height. It normally grows to about 1 m in height (or more in some cases) with a spread of about 1.5 m. The most commonly grown cultivar is *S. molloyi* 'Dragon's Gold' (56a,b), which has a long flowering season, lasting from late summer through to spring. (Hummock former)

***Sophora prostrata*** (56c) is the easiest species of kōwhai to identify. It has the smallest leaves (2.5 cm or less), is evergreen and has a tangled, divaricating habit of growth. It normally grows to between 1 and 2 m high. Its flowers, with orange-coloured outer petals, are usually less obvious than those of other species, being presented within the foliage. Its seed pods are also shorter than those of other species (up to 5 cm long). *S. prostrata* 'Little Baby' (56d) has yellow flowers. (Hummock former)

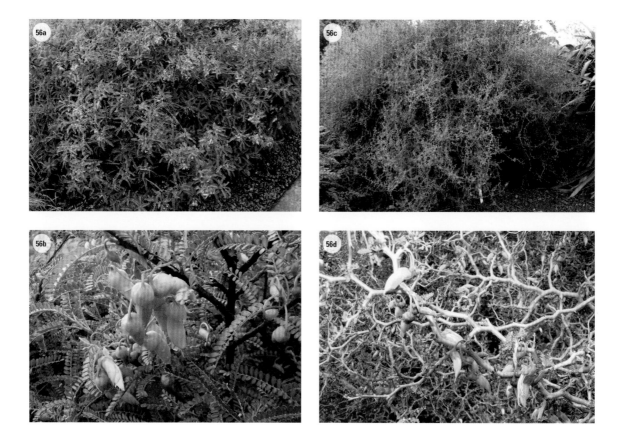

## 57. Uncinia

**Uncinia rubra** (57a) is a rather diminutive species of hook sedge, it seldom grows to more than about 35 cm tall, and it has fine leaves that are usually no more than 2 mm wide. It will form small, dense tufts of short, narrow leaves. (Clump former)

**Uncinia rubra 'Belinda's Find'** is a cultivar that forms a clump of grassy foliage up to 12 cm tall, purplish-red with bright-red variegation along the margins of each leaf. (Clump former)

## 58. Viola

**Viola cunninghamii** (58a) is a hardy, tufted perennial herb that grows well in a moist soil, in full sun or in shade. It flowers over much of the year and should be closely planted to ensure a good cover. (Carpet former)

## 59. Wahlenbergia

**Wahlenbergia albomarginata (New Zealand bluebell)** (59a) and **W. laxa** are two closely related species, one growing in the wetter mountain regions and the other growing mainly in the drier mountain regions. Both are deeply rooted, creeping perennials and they produce small rosettes of leaves just above the ground. Their flowers sit upright and their colour is quite variable – anything from white to a pale, flax blue, although the flower colour is quite stable depending on the parent stock. (Spreader)

# Glossary

**Air-filled porosity:** a measure of space between particles of medium, such as in a potting mix.

**Angiosperms (flowering plants):** seed plants whose ovules (undeveloped seeds) are enclosed by the ovary. *cf.* **Gymnosperms**

**Annual:** a plant that completes its life cycle within a calendar year. *See also* **Biennial**; **Perennial**

**Artificial selection:** plant selection by human intervention. *See also* **Cultivar**

**Axillary:** term applied to bud(s) in the axil of a leaf at the point of attachment to the stem.

**Biennial:** a plant that typically takes two years to complete its life cycle. *See also* **Annual**; **Perennial**

**Broadleaf weeds:** weeds other than narrow-leaved, grass-like species; mostly dicots.

**Budding:** a form of grafting that consists of a single bud and rootstock.

**Bulbs, corms:** modified storage stems or roots.

**Calyx (pl. calyces):** the outer whorl of parts of a flower, consisting of sepals.

**Carbohydrates:** the products of photosynthesis; sugars and starches.

**Carpet or mat formers:** plants that are more or less uniform in height and texture.

**Climax:** the end-point of succession. *See also* **Colonising plants; Natural succession**

**Clones:** plants with the same genotype, usually vegetatively propagated.

**Clump formers:** plants that increase in size from the base and are variable in height.

**Colonising plants:** plants that invade and outgrow smaller existing plants. *See also* **Climax**; **Natural succession**

**Cotyledons:** the first seed leaves of flowering plants and conifers.

**Cross-pollination:** pollen from a different flower than that which produces the seed.

**Crown:** condensed root and stem tissue at ground level.

**Cultivar:** a name given to a clonal line of plants maintained through artificial selection. *See also* **Hybrid**; **Variety**

**Cutting:** a form of vegetative propagation, usually using a piece of the stem, buds or leaves.

**Deciduous:** plants that normally lose their leaves and become dormant in the winter. *cf.* **Evergreen**

**Dioecious:** a plant that has either male or female flowers only. *cf.* **Monoecious**

**Divaricating:** a plant that branches at wide angles and that appears to grow in a tangled way.

**Division:** a form of plant propagation that often consists of dividing a plant at the crown.

**Dormancy:** having a resting or non-active phase.

**Evergreen:** having leaves that are retained and stay green throughout the year. *cf.* **Deciduous**

**Ferns:** a group of spore-bearing, non-flowering plants that often grow in moist, shady places. *See also* **Liverworts**; **Mosses**

**Fertilisers:** a substance used to supply nutrients required for plant growth. Fertilisers may be chemical or organic. *See also* **Slow-release fertiliser**

**Fronds:** the spore-bearing or sterile (barren) leaves of ferns.

**Fruits:** the product of the ripened ovaries of flowers; they contain seeds.

**Fungicide:** a chemical formulation used to kill fungal diseases.

**Gamete:** a male or female germ cell produced during sexual reproduction.

**Genus:** the first part of a binomial name.

**Germination:** the state when a seed or spore begins to grow.

**Glaucous:** blue-grey bloom, often powdery or waxy, usually occurring on leaves.

**Grafting:** the joining of two plant parts (a rootstock and scion) to create a single plant.

**Gymnosperms:** seed plants whose ovules (undeveloped seeds) are exposed; for example conifers. *cf.* **Angiosperms**

**Hardwood cutting:** a cutting taken from dormant, mature stems. *cf.* **Semi-ripe cutting**; **Softwood cutting**

**Herbaceous:** relating to plants or plant parts that are non-woody. *See also* **Woody plants**

**Herbicides:** chemicals used to kill weeds. There are many different types, with different modes of action; some are selective in killing just grasses, others kill just broadleaf weeds.

**Hummock formers:** bun-shaped plants planted close together that form ground cover.

**Hybrid:** the offspring of a cross between two different genera, species or varieties. *See also* **Cultivar**; **Variety**

**Internode:** the area between the nodes. *See also* **Node**

**Interspecific hybrids:** a hybrid cross between two or more species, usually from the same genus.

**Layering:** a form of vegetative propagation. A layer is similar to a cutting, but is still attached to the mother plant until it forms its own roots.

**Lignin:** a substance in the cell walls of many plants that gives woody plants their rigidity.

**Liverworts:** low-growing plants, mainly found in moist areas, which have no true stems or vascular system, no flowers or fruits, and that reproduce by spores. Liverworts often have a flattish appearance and generally there is no real distinction between root, stem and leaf, except in the so-called leafy liverworts. *See also* **Mosses**

**Macro-nutrients:** elements (other than carbon, hydrogen and oxygen) required by plants in substantial amounts; for example, nitrogen, phosphorus, potassium and calcium. *cf.* **Micro-nutrients**

**Micro-nutrients:** elements required by plants only in small amounts; for example boron, manganese, copper and zinc. *cf.* **Macro-nutrients**

**Monoecious:** plants that have separate male and female flowers on the same plant. *cf.* **Dioecious**

**Mosses:** low-growing plants, mainly found in moist areas, which have no true stems or vascular system, no flowers or fruits and reproduce by spores. Mosses tend to have tiny leaf-like structures and often appear velvet-like from a distance, often in varying shades of green or other colours depending on the species. *See also* **Liverworts**

**Mulch:** any form of organic or inorganic material applied to the soil surface.

**Natural succession:** the change in plant species in an area over time. *See also* **Climax**; **Colonising plants**

**Node:** a point on a stem where buds and leaves arise. *See also* **Internode**

**Non-organic material:** material that is not derived from living organisms; for example chemical fertilisers. *cf.* **Organic material**

**Organic material:** material derived from living organisms such as plants and animals. *cf.* **Non-organic material**

**Pellicle:** a thin, skin-like covering, as seen on the leaves of some *Astelia* species.

**Perennial:** a plant that lives for three years or more; it may be woody or herbaceous. *See also* **Annual**; **Biennial**

**Petiole:** the stalk of a leaf.

**pH:** a scale used to indicate acidity (below 7) or alkalinity (above 7) levels; a soil with a pH of 7 is neutral.

**Pinnae:** the primary divisions of a compound leaf or fern frond.

**Pinnate:** feather-like; used to describe the leaflets on a rachis.

**Pinnately compound leaf:** a single leaf with a leaf blade that is divided up like a feather.

**Pollination:** pollen attaching to female parts, starting the process of fertilisation in seed plants.

**Prostrate:** lying flat; plants that grow along the ground rather than upwards.

**Provenance:** the origin, area or environment where plants naturally grow and that influences seed selection.

**Raceme:** a type of flowering branch where the first flower to open is at the base of the stem.

**Rachis:** the extension of a pinnately compound leaf or frond beyond the petiole.

**Re-vegetation:** the reintroduction of native plants to an area.

**Rhizome:** a type of (mainly) underground stem.

**Root trainer:** a plant pot with vertical ribs and holes to prevent roots circling inside.

**Rooting hormones:** mainly synthetic auxins used to encourage adventitious root formation in cuttings.

**Rootstock:** the lower part of a composite plant. *See also* **Scion**

**Rosette:** leaves of a plant that radiate from the centre, close to the ground (e.g. dandelion).

**Scarify:** to scratch or cut the seed coat to allow water absorption in order to overcome dormancy.

**Scion:** the upper part of a composite plant. *See also* **Rootstock**

**Seed:** the product of fertilisation of flowering plants and gymnosperms (mainly conifers); may contain stored food. *See also* **Spore**

**Seed dormancy:** mechanisms that inhibit germination of viable seeds.

**Semi-ripe cutting:** a cutting taken from partially mature stems. *cf.* **Hardwood cutting**; **Softwood cutting**

**Sepals:** the outer layer of the parts of a flower that combine to make up the calyx.

**Shrubs:** woody plants that generally branch from the base and are smaller than most trees.

**Slow-release fertiliser:** encapsulated fertiliser; the rate of release is temperature related.

**Softwood cutting:** a cutting taken from soft, new growth. *cf.* **Hardwood cutting; Semi-ripe cutting**

**Species:** a basic level of classification for living organisms. Each species is normally capable of reproducing with others of its kind. A species normally has two parts to its name: a generic and a specific epithet (name).

**Sporangium (pl. sporangia):** a spore-bearing organ.

**Spore:** a simple, asexual, single-celled reproductive body produced by plants such as mosses, liverworts and ferns.

**Sprawlers:** a category of ground cover plants that have uneven growth forms.

**Spreaders:** a category of ground cover plants that spread by underground stems.

**Stipe:** the stalk of a fern frond (generally equivalent to a petiole).

**Stipites:** the stalks of leaflets (pinnae) within a compound leaf (frond) of a fern.

**Stolons:** stems that spread more or less parallel to, and above, the ground.

**Stratification:** a period of moist, cool chilling required by some plants or seeds.

**Sub-shrub:** a shrub that is not fully woody; partly herbaceous.

**Succulents:** plants with fleshy parts.

**Systemic herbicides:** chemicals that kill plants by being translocated through the sap system of actively growing plants.

**Tissue culture:** propagation of plants from a single cell or a few cells in a specialised facility and that results in clonal plants.

**Tomentum:** a woolly type of hair found on some plants.

**Transpiration:** the movement of water through a plant from the roots to the leaves and into the atmosphere.

**Undulate:** wavy, up and down (in reference to the edge of a leaf blade).

**Variety:** a minor morphological variation of a species that arises naturally. *See also* **Cultivar; Hybrid**

**Vegetative propagation:** any form of propagation that does not involve seeds or spores (e.g. cuttings, layers).

**Viability:** the ability of a seed to be able to germinate.

**Weed:** a plant growing where it is not wanted.

**Woody plants:** plants with lignified tissue; for example trees, shrubs and some climbing plants.

**Wrenching:** the process of cutting roots in advance of shifting an established plant.

# Sources of New Zealand native ground cover plants

Diack's Nurseries Ltd, 849 North Road, Makarewa, Invercargill 9876
www.diacks.co.nz

Fern Factor, 394 Newtons Rd, RD5, Christchurch
www.fernfactor.co.nz

Hains Horticulture, Simpson Road, RD4, Wanganui

Home Creek Nursery, 295 Hillside Road, Manapouri, Te Anau 9679
www.homecreeknursery.co.nz

Joy Plants, 78 Jericho Rd, RD2, Pukekohe
www.joyplants.co.nz

Kapiti Nursery online wholesale and retail
www.kapitinursery.co.nz

Matai Nurseries, 52 Harris Street, Waimate 7924
www.nznatives.co.nz

Moores Valley Nurseries, 285 Moores Valley Road, Wainuiomata; or 132 McLeavey Rd, Ohau, Levin
www.mooresvalleynurseries.co.nz

Motukarara Conservation Nursery, Waihora Park, Motukarara, Christchurch
www.doc.govt.nz

Naturally Native Nursery, Tauranga Head Office, 30 Gamman Mill Road, Oropi, RD3, Tauranga; and
Naturally Native Nursery, 65 Keepa Road, Whakatane
www.naturallynative.co.nz

Oratia Native Plant Nursery, 625 West Coast Road, Oratia, Auckland
www.oratianatives.co.nz

Ribbonwood Nurseries, corner of Glenelg and Ronay Streets, Bradford, Dunedin
www.ribbonwoodnurseries.co.nz

Taupo Wholesale Gardens Centre, 155 Centennial Drive, Taupo
www.tauponativeplant.co.nz

Titoki Nursery, 26 Palmer Road, Waimea West, Nelson
www.titokinursery.co.nz

Trees for Canterbury, 42 Charlesworth Street, Woolston, Christchurch
www.treesforcanterbury.org.nz

Tree Guys Nursery, 4 Higginson Street, Otane, Central Hawke's Bay
www.treeguysnursery.co.nz

# Useful references

Boddy, F. A. 1974. *Groundcover and Other Ways to Weed-free Gardens.* David and Charles (Holdings) Ltd, Newton Abbot, Devon, UK.

Brownsey, P. J. and Smith-Dodsworth, J. C. 1989. *New Zealand Ferns and Allied Plants.* David Bateman Ltd, Auckland.

Cobham, R. 1975. *Amenity Landscape Management.* E. & F. N. Spon, London, UK.

Crowe, A. 1994. *Which Native Fern?* Viking Penguin Books (NZ) Ltd, Auckland.

Fisher, M. 1984. *Gardening with New Zealand Ferns.* Collins, Auckland.

Harrington, K. C. & Schmitz. H. K. 2007. Initial screening of herbicides tolerated by native plants. *New Zealand Plant Protection* 60:133–136.

Metcalf, L. J. 1991. *The Cultivation of New Zealand Trees and Shrubs.* Reed Books, Auckland.

Metcalf, L. J. 1993. *The Cultivation of New Zealand Native Plants.* Godwit Press Ltd, Auckland.

Metcalf, L. J. 1998. *The Cultivation of New Zealand Grasses.* Random House, Auckland.

Popay, I., Champion, P. & James, T. 2010. *An Illustrated Guide to Common Weeds of New Zealand* (3rd edition). New Zealand Plant Protection Society, Lincoln.

Thomas, G. S. 1977. *Plants for Ground Cover* (rev. edition). J. M. Dent and Sons, London, UK.

Van de Spuy, U. 1976. *Gardening with Groundcovers.* A. H. & A. W. Reed, Wellington.

Young, S. (editor) 2009. *New Zealand Novachem Agrichemical Manual.* AgriMedia Ltd, Christchurch.

# Index of New Zealand native ground cover plants

Page numbers in **bold** refer to illustrations.